FAIRWAYS!
What Fairways?

FAIRWAYS!
What Fairways?

ALFIE AND HARRY WARD

To order additional copies of this book, contact:
Xlibris LLC
0-800-056-3182
www.xlibrispublishing.co.uk
Orders@xlibrispublishing.co.uk
306510

Contents

Fairways! What Fairways? 11

Once Upon a Time—In Roberton Village 25

Sunday Golf and the Sabbath Observance 39

Build It—and the People Will Come! 43

The Restoration Begins—For Real 50

The Joys of Gutta-percha 60

The Importance of Golf 65

Tourism, Revenge, and Twa' Puddocks! 72

Golf's Dilemma—the Ball! 89

Forever Chasing Rainbows and Funding 94

Dreams, Disinfectant, and Compensation 108

Stars, Pros, Saints, and Sinners 121

Every One a Star! 127

Unearthing the Soul of Golf 145

Guid Folk, Ne'er-do-wells, and Coos 158

All Balls, but Nae Courage 169

Ashes to Ashes 178

Never Say Never. The Chase Goes On! 182

A Field Is a Field Is a Field Is a Field 196

Don't Be Bitter—Be Careful... 202

Timeline of Clydesdales Golf Courses 209

Bibliography 211

Acknowledgements 213

"Golf is a science, a study of a lifetime in which you may exhaust yourself, but never your subject. It is a contest, a duel or a melee, calling for skill, strategy and self control. It is a test of temper, a trial of honour, a revealer of character. It affords the chance to play the man and act the gentleman".

Robert Forgan 1824-1900

We dedicate this book to our mother, Margaret Ward,
who taught all of us (and many others) the 'right' way in life.
Hoping you found your God!

Fairways! What Fairways?

Perhaps it's time, I'm thinking. On a bleak September Saturday afternoon, it is the finale to another bleak and crappish summer, and the Scottish weather doesn't usually get much better from here on in! I suppose that's the price you pay for living in such a beautiful country. Watching the TV coverage of the Walker Cup eases the discomfort of a somewhat solemn mood, and I'm really thinking . . . Aye! Perhaps it *is* time?

Having just recently opened an interesting email conversation with an American golfer regarding the curious properties of an olde worlde material called gutta-percha, I feel sensations of stirring adrenalin in the veins once more. Chris McIntyre is another hickory golf enthusiast, one of genuine guys, who makes his own replica guttas, just like Harry and I did on this side of the pond a few years back.

Having traded each other's samples and information across the pond, memories and aspirations are easily rekindled by the mere mention of making gutta-percha golf balls. Aye! It's high time we wrote the bloody book on Arbory Braes—a wee golf course adventure, which had more than just one twist to it, on which Harry and I had embarked at the end of the twentieth century.

We go back a long way, Harry and I. Then, of course, we would as we're the two youngest brothers of five, plus one solitary sister. All of us born into a wonderful family, and all so lucky health wise throughout our lives, it has to be said. Harry and I shared many pursuits in our youthful years—football in particular. We must have (shamefully) broken most of mum's ornaments playing indoor fitba' on winter days during our childhood years!

Into our teenage years and it was the misspent youth syndrome of playing endless hours of snooker during the winter months that we both became fairly decent. Harry was more accomplished at billiards whereas my forte was the potting of balls in snooker. Later still, we shared more pints of beer and tots of whisky that I care to mention, although sobriety is now the favoured option for both of us. I suppose you could say that we were kind of . . . joined at the hip? Ultimately, we both shared an obsession regarding golf from childhood right up to the present day—once more, with both of us achieving that magical single figure handicap. Ah, those were the days!

Then along came 1995, the year of Biggar golf clubs' centennial. By this time in modern golfing history, there were hundreds of golf clubs all over the UK celebrating 100 years of golf in their particular locality, courtesy of the so-called 'boom' years. Many were now entering into the occasion with great enthusiasm and vigour to honour their founder members while using it as a good excuse for some partying along the way.

Naturally, we delved into this jollification of golfing events with all guns blazing. Harry had accepted the captaincy of the club in 1994, and I was roped into the committee for brotherly back-up, having been evasive of such activity in the preceding twenty years. Oh, well, better late than never, and this was going to be a helluva busy time for all concerned.

The lead-up to 1995 saw Harry and I taking on what was intended to be the centenary brochure (amongst other things); the brochure turning into a handy wee book, predictably typical of the centennial variety. Our research had been expansive, to say the least, and very few stones were left unturned in the quest for historical information on the clubs in the past dating back to 1895.

It was the leftovers from this local golf history exercise that was to prove instrumental in steering both our futures. All sorts of 'stuff' had (surprisingly) popped out at us as we raked through the Biggar Museum Archive, local national libraries, newspaper articles via microfiche and also made doorstep visits, including a trip to Aberlady, near Gullane on the east coast of Scotland, to meet an incredible man by the name of Archie Baird.

It must have been around early 1994 when we first met Archie. We had befriended the St Andrian golf historian and reincarnation of Tom Morris Sr, David Joy, as part of the Biggar golf club centenary celebrations. David had tipped us off about the whereabouts of Mr Baird and how he would probably be able and willing to help us with our research. So Harry phoned Archie to see if there was any way he could assist us with our continuing golf research. Archie's response was positive, decisive, and clear, when he said, 'You'd better get your backsides down here, and we'll see what we can muster up for you.'

We set off for Aberlady the next day full of anticipation of what we might get from Archie, whose wife Sheila is a direct descendant of Willie Park Sr of Musselburgh, who in turn was the first ever winner of the Championship Belt at Prestwick in 1860 and twice in 1863 and 1866 before young Tom Morris claimed it for his own by winning the Belt three times in succession from 1868 to 1870. Park Sr would go on to win the Claret Jug in 1875, again at Prestwick. His son, Willie Park Jr, was one of the deadliest putters of his day and uttered some of the truest words in golf when he said, '*The man who can putt is a match for anyone!*'

We were like two wee boys heading off to a favourite aunt, in the hope of cadging some chocolate sweeties or perhaps even a toffee apple if we were really lucky! Having arrived in this Mecca of pure golfing heaven with a multitude of great courses spread in every direction, virtually each one on the other's doorstep all along the east coast of Scotland, we found the wee man's door and gave it a good rattle. The door opened instantly, and the rugged voice assumed correctly, 'You must be the Ward brothers from Biggar? Come away in.'

As soon as we reached the living room, Archie left us in no doubt about that day's procedure. 'I must apologise, boys. I've got a match at Kilspindie in half an hour, so I hope you'll understand that we have to be quick!' he said briskly, but politely. We simply nodded our approval and understanding at such comments. God knows how many times Harry and I had been rushing at the last minute to make our tee off time for the Saturday Medal or some match, so we fully understood the situation. He then continued to give us a brief introduction into some of the impressive collection of memorabilia he had gathered over the years before hurriedly stating, 'But this stuff's nae use to you, guys. What you want is up in my study. If you'll follow me, gents.'

We'd hardly spoken a word between us as we followed Archie upstairs, keeping close so as not to waste time! 'Right then!' Archie exclaimed. 'What was it you're researching again? Lanarkshire?' He paused for a moment, looking at the rows of books on the shelves. 'Hmm? We'll need something to put them in. I'll be back in a moment.'

As he left the room, leaving Harry and me agog at what we were looking at, Harry whispered to me, 'Christ's sake, this is better than the Mitchell Library!' At which point, Archie hastily re-entered the study with a large cardboard box that made my heart palpitate in anticipation at the size of it! Surely he wasn't going to fill this bloody box with golfing literature antiquities?

'OK. You'll need a Golf Annual . . . Oh bugger it, you'd better take the whole lot!' He started to load the box, periodically glancing round over his shoulder at us to get some indication of which ones we wanted. The world was our oyster! As he dislodged each book, he looked for a nod of approval before dispatching it hurriedly into that big cardboard box that had reached saturation point at the blink of an eye! 'Ah, Stirk and Henderson's *Golf in the Making*—you'll definitely want that one!'

Archie had a match to play, and we were holding him back. By the look of that box and its contents, we were going to be very busy copying over the next few days or weeks! The box was full to the brim with golfing literature, and we said our appreciative farewells to Archie so that he could get off to his game of golf. We shook hands, and as we started to walk away, Archie declared in characteristically gruff fashion, '*Strength to your arm, boys! Strength to your arm!*'

We got back to the van and popped the box on the back seat. 'Jesus Christ, Harry! Do you realise what we've got there?' I said.

He gave a laugh and replied, 'Aye, we could nip away for a guid wee golfing holiday on that lot!' In Archie, we had found an incredibly sincere and genuine golf historian—someone who appreciated golf's fine history and was prepared to help and trust others who wanted to learn about the game's voluminous past. We would be seeing more of Archie in the future.

Now we had both been wise to the fact that golf had been played at the nearby villages of Crawford, Symington, Leadhills, Broughton, and Thankerton, which were, by now, totally defunct and almost forgotten in living memory with the exception of Leadhills. Then on various obscure days at some library . . . 'Did ye ken they hud a course at Tarbrax?'

'Naw. Ah didnae ken that.'

'Ah've got wan fur Roberton playin' Abington in a match!'

'Whit aboot Douglas?'

'Douglas?!'

'Aye, Douglas!'

'Yer bloody kiddin' me!'

Such was the pitch between two highly enthusiastic and erudite researchers—short to the point and lacking in a little vocabulary. At this stage, one thing was for sure—we were well and truly smitten by the golf history bug.

I can just imagine thousands of Americans, English, Dutch, German . . . whatever . . . golfers and non-golfers, trying to decipher the Scots tongue in this book, for which I make no apology whatsoever. There's always the incredible 'Google' to fall back on if a translation is required. This recalls me of the hilarious sketch by Robin Williams, in one of his live shows, and his take on the inventors of golf—the Scots. He takes the mickey out of our indecipherable accents and our use of the Scots language. It is perhaps a bit strong in the language stakes for some, but absolutely hilarious just the same!

Whether we, as Scots, had actually invented this sport from the very spirit of its core doesn't really matter. We, as Scots, were undeniably responsible for bringing it forth to what it is today! Golf? It's *our* game! And being the true humanitarians that we are, we shared it with the rest of the world. '*It's nae loss, what a freend gets!*' However, the home of golf is *not* a solitary place or country—it's a *planet!*

Also, I'm reminded of a discussion group at the best golf web site I've ever came across—www.golfclubatlas.com, where the majority of the posters are Americans. Don't you just love them?! Big fat baldy drummer is a native of Fife, and being a Scot in 'Burns' week, he posted an off topic thread of a Burns verse to commemorate the great bard. Big lanky bummer, here, saw the post and responded in some broad Scots dialect. Thereafter, we both interacted in a language that only Scots can understand. Some poor guy came across our discussion and stated, 'Hey, you guys. Don't have a fucking clue what you're talking about, but it sure sounds interesting and has a certain rhyme to it.'

All this *stuff*—what use was it and what could we do with it? It probably amounted to the equivalent of a good tree in paper manufacture—copies of newspaper articles, book extracts, medal results, and course sketches of golf in rural Clydesdale and elsewhere. One thing was for sure, it would have to be set aside for the present, until we had seen the back of a centenary year that went down like a mean fart in a fully occupied lift!

Don't get me wrong; the committee worked bloody hard, most of them, and there was a hard core of supportive members doing their bit. But the usual apathy was the norm, and almost everything we tried to organise became a tough sell. Something we would experience on a national level later on?

Winter of 1995 was now approaching, and we'd both been scunnered with our highest expectations turning slightly sour. It had been a long haul, and we were now drifting like two autumnal leaves floating aimlessly up the first fairway of Biggar golf course on the first floodwaters of winter. No big fallout—just a parting of the ways, and it was time for Harry and me to move on. Just like Scotland should!

The present and third course at Biggar had been built upon what was historically termed as 'the bogs of Biggar' in 1907. This low-lying ground had been reclaimed from 1817 onwards by an extensive drainage scheme. No surprise then that winter golf here is reminiscent of the seaside links, except there's hardly any grass to play off, and if there was, you'd need the Nigg ferry to get you round the eighteen! To be fair, it's still a very pleasant round in the summer months though. Maybe they should have stayed on higher and better draining ground at Langlees in 1895?

Now that we'd seen off our civic duties for club and golf, we found ourselves free and independent. Just like Scotland should be! With nobody to hold us back, we were now a two-man committee where a casting vote was never required, with golf remaining very high on the agenda, golf history in its true homeland. During periods of extensive hours of research, usually at The Mitchell Library, we'd have our periodical tea and fag breaks.

Reflecting upon that day's work with, sometimes, very little to show for the effort, I would say, 'What the bloody hell are we doing this for? What's the point?'

And Harry would reply optimistically, 'Ach. Ye canny do all this work without something good coming out of it. I really believe that!'

A little eye contact in a moment of silent pondering, flick the dog ends, and then back we would go to our labour of love—searching for golf-related 'stuff'. Some ten years on and the marvels of the Internet now allow the researcher, sometimes, to plod away quietly in the comfort of their own living room! Sometimes . . . no, most times, modern technologies have their place in life—but the ruling bodies should have pulled the reins on hot ball technology decades ago!

There was still so much to learn and discover about golf, especially that of the inland variety. Some people say that inland golf isn't really true golf. Silly numpties that they are! If it hadn't been for the evolution of the inland variety, then the sport would only be a shadow of itself today.

Even here in Clydesdale golf took off during the 1890s, as it would around the whole of Britain, America, and elsewhere, in what is termed as the boom years of golf. We had in our possession these newspaper sketches of long gone courses right on our doorstep. Little maps of the hole layouts with various clues as to where the bloody things were located. We really needed to go out and find ourselves some defunct golf courses! And that's exactly what we did, and with fervour and enthusiasm.

So I suppose this is the point where our research became more physical. And through this physicality, we soon found ourselves making the news in the local gazette courtesy of all our gallivanting around the countryside. I think it was as early as this that we were being touted as the first *golf course archaeologists* and won our first minute of fame! Stretching it somewhat, but hey, we can hack that sort of publicity.

Site visits had already been made to the ghostly golfing fields of Biggar, Broughton, Tarbrax, Carluke, Thankerton, Symington, Douglas, Coalburn, Lesmahagow, Abington, Roberton, Leadhills, and the jewel in the crown—Crawford.

Crawford was special due to the fact that it had eighteen holes in 1888, as opposed to all the others having only nine. It was also laid out by none other than Old Tom Morris of St Andrews with some able assistance from the forward-thinking local minister, the Reverend Christopher McKune. Even the distinguished Lanark club, the twenty-fifth oldest golf club in the world founded in 1851, only had a layout of fourteen holes in 1888. McKune had laid out nine holes on what was his kirk glebe prior to 1888. A church glebe was a piece of land, usually a few acres, which a minister would have at his disposal to do with as he pleased, in order to generate some extra income.

Part of the itinerary on all of these scouting missions included the taking of photos and sometimes video footage of these vacant landscapes. While surveying the Crawford course we had in our possession a monochrome postcard showing the entire course from the elevated position of a nearby hill named Ritchieferrie. Oh well, we'd better try and find out exactly where this photographer took his shots from and see the panoramic view for ourselves, we thought.

So we drove over to the other side of the village and parked at the bottom of Ritchieferrie. The first few hundred yards were a slight ascent until we met the bottom of the real hill. Then it got tougher. Much tougher! The climb was near bloody vertical for about 300 feet, and by the time we reached less steep ground, we were both completely buggered. We persevered for another 200 feet or so, then plunked our arses down on the nearly dry grass of the slope, and you've guessed it—we had a fag.

Ah, aren't such treks so worthwhile when the visual reward is before your eyes? We'd successfully retraced the photographer's footsteps and took dozens of our own pictures of the surrounding scenery, including, of course, some of the golf course sitting elevated high above the village of Crawford. It was here in Crawford at the end of the twelfth century that William Wallace had slain a few English and burnt the garrison to the ground to avenge the murder of his wife, Marion! Thankfully for us, this didn't include any of our own ancient ancestors, or we wouldn't be here to tell the story. Come to think of it, our paternal ancestors would have been Irish at this time.

Quite a while later, we decided that another trip up the hill was required because some of the original pictures hadn't turned out to be very good. We didn't have the benefit of the modern digital camera in those days. It was a tiresome thought to scale that bloody cliff face again, and we knew that there was a service road that went right to the top of the hill where a telecommunication mast was located. So long as the gate at the bottom wasn't padlocked, our quid was in. It wasn't locked! I got out of the van to open the gate and then jumped back in.

'Listen, Harry. Have you seen the guys going up here before? Don't they use a four by four?'

'Naw. They've jeest got an ordinary van like this,' he assured me.

'Oh well, let's go for it then. The weather could turn on us any time.'

It was early winter, and although there hadn't been any snow to speak of, it was bloody cold and icy. The road we were ascending was a simple single track that had been dug out of the stony hillside. It wasn't long before we heard the familiar sound of the sump scraping against the ground below our feet. Higher and higher we climbed, crawling in first gear and dodging small loose boulders as we progressed! What excitement!

This might not have been our best idea to date as there was little chance of turning back now. Then, because we had climbed so high, the road appeared to be showing signs of the white stuff, and sure enough the wee van started to slip on ice and we ground to a halt! Shit! What do we do now? Luckily for us, we had just passed a slightly wider area in the road about twenty yards back, and I do mean, *slightly* wider. Harry could just be able to use all his driving skills and do a ten-point turn to get us facing downhill again.

Back we went, ever so slowly, and carefully, and he started to lock the steering round . . . 'Jeest hold on, Harry. You'll have to be bloody careful or you'll be over the side! I'll get out and guide you, because there's no point in both of us getting killed!'

'Very funny, ya big bastard!' was his curt reply. After some seven or eight manoeuvres, he managed to turn the van and all was well again. So he aimed the van into the side of the hill as a precaution against having a runaway train and parked up. Blocking the road wasn't a concern to offending other road users on Ritchieferrie hill–I mean, how many idiots are there out there? We then, quite casually made our way round the hillside to take our pictures.

That wee van took us to many places, but that was the hairiest experience to date! We didn't hang about after the photo shoot as a quick fall of snow then could have brought disastrous consequences. There were no salt gritters on this piece of track. We made our descent and made it safely to the bottom of the hill where we both gave a moderate sigh of relief.

'I was really worried when you had to turn the van, Harry,' I said with brotherly sincerity.

'Were ye?' he asked in amazement.

'Oh, aye. Ah thought I was going to have to walk all the way home if you'd gone over the side!' I said, laughing. Off we went, heading for home, laughing and joking all the way. Could anyone ever know how exciting and amusing, and surprisingly dangerous, golf research can be?

These inquisitive forays into the lands that golf forgot led to endless questions being volleyed back and forth with (sometimes) only supposition supplying possible answers. I find it quite amazing that information from a mere century back can be impossible to procure, while my brother Tam can learn so much from archaeological samples dating back thousands of years!

Of course, we didn't have sketches for every golf course, so there was a lot of foot trudging, and some amateur detective work had to be done in order to try and locate the right *fields*. Sometimes we found a farming legacy of intrinsic golf information passed down through the generations; . . . 'Hello, we're looking for the auld golf course,' we'd enquire from the farmer.

'Och. That'll be the gowf course "field" jeest up yonder' would be the reply. Simple!

On the more evading side of procuring information, we found a familiar response when knocking doors. 'Hello. We're looking for information regarding the old golf course that used to be around here—somewhere. Can you help?'

'Nah. But auld Wullie wid ken a' aboot it,' would be a general reply.

'Ah. So where does Wullie stay?'

'Och. He's been deid fur years now!'

Whether it was Wullie or Jimmy, Peter, Mary, or Norma—and regardless of what area we were researching, this response became matter of fact, and we soon realised that we were about twenty years too late in getting our act together with Clydesdale's golf research!

Actual evidence of a long gone course is difficult to find using eyesight alone. Nature soon reclaims her own except where those ancient golfers had to manually excavate greens and tees into hillside slopes as we found on the Broadlaw at Leadhills which were tiny, and then quite impressively on Midhill at Crawford, thanks to the substantial size of the Crawford greens.

And the remnants of these archaic courses are still visible for all to see today. The only problem at Crawford is the bloody M74 motorway that some stupid buggers drove right through the middle of that course in the 1960s! Come to think of it, I believe Dad worked on that motorway! That's progress, I suppose?

Going back to the Broadlaw course at Leadhills, I remember Harry falling foul of a little accident, as he was prone to do. We had been up on the hill inspecting the tiny tees and greens that had been cut into the hillside and were heading back down to the car on the roadside below. There was a steep banking to descend which had been sprinkled by a heavy shower ten minutes earlier.

As Harry started his descent, he lost his footing and slumped on to his arse with a good old bump, and the slight momentum he had generated helped him to get to the bottom a lot quicker than he had anticipated. 'Ouch! Oh, oh. Aghhhh!' Down he went on this twenty-five-foot, near-perpendicular slide in two and a half seconds. What fun!

When I got to the bottom of the slope, in a more conventional and sensible manner to join him, I was in raptures of laughter at his misfortune, which wasn't appreciated very much. His black muck-laden arse was soaking and probably bruised for all I knew, and a pair of his best trousers was destined for the bucket! I really shouldn't have laughed—but I did!

Along with actually finding these lost stretches of sporting land, we'd go door knocking in the quest for more information. Top strategy there was to find the auldest auld bugger in each area. As far as Tarbrax was concerned, this little ploy didn't quite work out as planned. Mrs Wilson had long since received the Queen's telegram for reaching the century mark, and she remained as bright as a button when we made our visit to her door (somewhat apprehensively due to her age). But she had lived in the village of Tarbrax her entire life! Whoopee! A dream catch for any researcher, you would think . . .

'Ah can remember seein' the golfers walkin' up the road there wae thir clubs under their airms, headin' fur the course. But ah didnae play golf, nor did ah ken anythin' aboot them.'

In Mrs Wilson we had found a real live one—but a complete dud for golf. That was the extent of her knowledge of golf in Tarbrax circa 1914 to the early twenties, which confirmed where the course actually was, but alas, not a morsel more, bless her! We sat and blethered with her for a couple of hours, listening to her recall her past years, and there were plenty of them!

Eventually, she received a jovial ticking off for failing to share an interest in golf in her early life, but she promised to 'take it up' if reincarnated. I even thought she was going to swipe me with her sweeping brush for having the cheek and audacity to suggest that I should make the cup of tea when we visited her.

'Ah might be auld, but ah can still mak' a cup of tea, son!' I was told bluntly. Long gone now, like so many worthies and like so many golf courses! *Tempus fugit*. These were fun moments, and we had plenty of them. The banter, you see. Oh, the banter!

There was one day when Harry and I were out and about doing some field surveys. We'd decided to go to Carluke that day and investigate one of the early courses there on the grounds of Langshaw farm. That was Carluke's second course laid out in 1894, the first being at the bottom end of Carluke on the grounds of Whitehill and Belstane in 1893. Having survived our introduction to the farmer and his less than friendly farm dogs—I nearly shit myself when they bounced off the van, barking mad, when we drove into the farmyard! Nice welcoming party, but mercifully, the farmer himself was friendly enough.

Anyway, we walked all over the grounds in the hope of finding some modicum of past golfing evidence. Perhaps an old teeing ground (usually no bigger than a good-sized living room carpet) or even better the levellings of an old green (sometimes no bigger than the living room itself, or maybe, just maybe . . . we would unearth a hidden gem in the shape of an old lost golf ball, preferably a gutta-percha)

Every time we set out on such missions, Harry would declare (ad nauseam) his intent of finding such a treasure, and the idea was perfectly plausible as most of Clydesdale's earliest courses were laid out at the back end of the gutty era. So, not wanting to disappoint (in the name of brotherly love), I had been patiently scheming a plot for quite a while. All I needed was an opportune moment in which to carry out the scurrilous, but well-intentioned plan. The time had arrived!

For weeks, I had been carrying an old scuffed-up, and worthless, early 1920s Dunlop lattice pattern ball in my pocket just waiting for the right moment. It is not to be confused with the great Dunlop 65 from 1934 onwards, when the '65' was added in commemoration of Henry Cotton's first Open win in 1934 where he shot a fabulous 65 in his second round at Royal St George's. This old 'tattie' that I had was far more important as it was about to make someone very, very happy . . . albeit perhaps, momentarily.

We had decided to head home after a few hours of walking about the place. Everything was heavily overgrown, and we hadn't learnt a lot about Carluke's second golf course this day. We approached a fairly steep banking rising to about ten feet, and I was leading the way.

Hmmm, this might do the business, I thought.

As Harry was directly behind me, right at my arse in fact, I deliberately stumbled as though losing my footing on the banking, while at the same time conveniently placing the ball on the ground for him to see, hopefully. 'Watch yersel. It's bloody slippy there,' I told him as I made it to the top. Sure enough, the bait had been swallowed!

'Ha ha, ho ho! Ye walked right ower it and never bloody saw it!' he exclaimed victoriously.

'Saw what?'

'This!' And he showed me the ball when I turned round to acknowledge his triumph. At this instant I had to choke back the first chortle before sharing my fraudulent excitement at such a find. We talked about it for a couple of minutes, examined it for historical details, and took a photo to authenticate the relic just for good measure. By now, I just had to look forward and start walking away, because my sides were nearly bursting with internal laughter that desperately wanted to escape.

Having walked another fifty yards, me leading and Harry babbling away in the background, we came to a fence. Once over the fence, Harry re-emphasised his ecstasy in getting one over me, and then I simply broke down and started to vomit laughter.

'What are ye laughing at?' Then there was a short pause before the penny dropped with a devastating clunk.

'Nah, ye didnae? . . . Ya big bastard! What a rotten thing tae do. Ah'll never forgive ye, ya big rotten bastard!'

By now, I was way out of control, and that old Dunlop ball found its way whizzing past my left ear as fast as a ferocious shank with a three iron! I don't think he intended to miss. We got to the van and made for home, Harry remonstrating all the way, and me, well, my conscience was beginning to tell me I had gone too far on this one and the atmosphere was frosty, to say the least. But Christ—it was funny! There would be payback for this little prank. That much was for sure.

Once Upon a Time—In Roberton Village

The research and the field surveys continued week after week till we decided to go and have a look at Roberton's first course on the lands of Hillend farm in early spring of 1997. The village is situated about six miles south of Biggar.

Beith Forrest was a local councillor and farmer of these grounds, and as courtesy would have it, we took ourselves up to the farm to speak with Beith and hopefully get his blessing to roam around the golf course fields. This was attained without any fuss, and we proceeded to the course to begin our survey. We're lucky in Scotland as there isn't any trespass law in the open spaces as such, so consent isn't really required because we have what is now called 'freedom to roam'. But it's still courteous to inform the farmers or landowners of what you're up to and essentially follow the countryside code!

In Roberton's golf course, we had the original sketch of the nine hole course dating back to 1892 complete with yardages amounting to a modest 1835 yards, so that exercise was relatively easy. Having walked over the course and predictably found absolutely nothing that resembled either tee or green, Harry noticed a small hill rising to about 100 feet above what once was the 5th fairway and green. By the way, the word 'fairway' derives from seafaring lingo meaning the navigable part of a river, harbour, etc., meaning *safe passage*.

Being the adventurers we are, we scaled this mountain, and to our eternal pleasure, we discovered a gorgeous view overlooking the defunct course and also a great view looking north, down the Clyde valley, past the village of Lamington, and towards Biggar. Clydesdale isn't a mountainous region of Scotland; it has more rolling hills and scenic glens of what is a small part of the Southern Uplands. Braveheart country!

You can almost be excused for getting lost in your own thoughts in such an environment. We sat there, high above a past golfing ground while happily puffing away at our fags, visualising old duffers sclaffing their way round with their mashies and niblicks, and then suddenly from nowhere a dream was born! The peace and tranquillity was shattered when out of the blue . . .

'What would it take tae lay this out again?' Harry asked.

'Eh? Are ye serious?'

'Aye. What would it take?' he insisted. The silence was resumed for a short while as we both gathered ourselves for the inevitable forthcoming discussion.

And then, there began the biggest brainstorming mission we had undertaken so far. Harry was definitely the instigator, with me, primarily, acting as the pessimist and doubting Thomas. But the more he talked about the possibilities, the more I began to believe in his crazy proposal: Anything is possible. You should never discount the possibilities—of an impossibility!

The idea was to restore the greens to some form of basic playability and try to involve a group of 'hickory' players who were fellow members of the British Golf Collectors Society to play it. Any funds we could raise would go to some worthwhile charity. The golfers in question were enthusiasts who played most of their golf with hickory-shafted golf clubs and got all dressed up in the old clobber for the occasion as well! Hmmm. Nae problem! We could do that, and it could be a host of fun too.

The seed had been sown. But before a single blow could be struck on this reclamation mission, we would have to secure a work permit, as this time we were going to be 'tampering' (albeit, ever so gently) with the land. Off we headed to Hillend farm to see Beith once more, and once more, he saw no problem with what we were proposing. Game on! So off we went to get ourselves organised for those charitable toils and labours ahead. All we really needed for the task were some basic hand tools: shovel, spade, fork, rake, and wheelbarrow!

We already knew exactly where the location of all the nine greens had been placed previously, courtesy of our little sketch of the course. Although reasonably flat, these areas would necessitate some initial form of brutal restoration work! Harry's wee electric garden hover mower would do the trick nicely, and as Harry also had access to an electric (petrol) Genny to boot the mower up, then all was in hand for the restoration of Roberton golf course. With regard to the materials required, we had the knowledge learnt from the lessons of none other than Old Tom Morris to thank for his ancient green-keeping wisdom.

Apparently, while carrying out some work on the Old Course at St Andrews in the early days with his assistant Honeyman, Tom noticed that the grass flourished where some sand had been spilled accidentally. Thereafter, Old Tom's cry would be heard on the course when working on the greens, 'Mair saund, Honeyman, mair saund!'

OK then, we'll get sand from the local quarry at Thankerton and cart it up in my ageing, but reliable, Bedford van. Coincidentally, the quarry lay at the top end of where the original Thankerton golf course was laid out in 1905. The course stretched down to the edge of the famous river Clyde. Numerous old balls have turned up over the years, courtesy of the quarry workings.

While on the subject of golf course restoration, I've always been bemused by the American philosophy of course restoration. Their enthusiasm for historical significance can only be admired, but in my book, if you want to restore a golf course to what its previous values were, then you'd have to restore the equipment values used at the point in time in that particular golf course.

Harry and I were planning a true restoration of an old defunct course of the 1890s to be played upon with the equipment of that same era—hickory clubs and gutta balls! Restoring the actual people who played the course was unrealistic and beyond our capabilities.

There was nothing to lose by experimenting on the Roberton course. The only financial outlay we had was for a couple of tons of coarse grit sand which I could get for about a couple of quid for half a ton! Everything else was our own time, effort, and sweat. And no permanent damage was being caused to the ground with regard to affecting Beith's grazing for his sheep. Another handy fact was the actual location of the course. It was fairly remote and free from any nosy onlookers who might embarrass us by questioning our sanity.

And so it came to pass that on 24 May 1997, on a rather cool but dry day, we ventured forth to the promised land of Ladygill, whereupon we would strike the first blows towards the resurrection of a long-lost hallowed green. At least it felt that way, for us. There we were, loaded up and parked up and rarin' to go!

First things first, though. Flasks were made ready for a wee quick cuppa, bread sandwich, and fag to finish. Once refreshed, we selected a reasonably even and level piece of ground which inclined slightly towards the approach shot, then kicked up the Genny and made a start on Roberton's original fifth green.

There was great hilarity between the intrepid green-keepers as stones, thistles, sheep shit, weeds, moss, and just a few morsels of grass succumbed to the fierce rotation of the hover mower's blade! Several humps on the surface were resisting all efforts to level them off, so we exposed them with a spade, which revealed bloody great boulders under the sward. Planetary movements had been pushing them up to the surface for almost a century! These were excavated and discarded to the side, leaving depressions that were teased back up the best we could with the fork.

Once the agreed area of a green had been decided upon, about twenty-five square yards in all, we tined the entire area with the fork and stood back to admire our handiwork. The general assessment was that the green was still in a generally crap condition! But we didn't have sand at the ready, so before we got too down in the dumps over our labours, we decided to try making an impression on the fourth and sixth greens before our enthusiasm showed signs of waning. After about five-hours' graft, we had the first three of the nine greens truly scalped! A good energetic start to an honourable cause.

The following weekend, we returned to do battle once more. The three greens that we'd made a start on had been exposed to a full week of dry, hot, sunny weather, and they still looked very uneven. But after we had given them another scalping with the hover mower and raked in a healthy coating of coarse sand, hey, hey, they were actually beginning to look the part! Don't forget that this exercise wasn't about recreating a manicured replica of blade-perfect Augusta National. There would be no room or time spent on tricking up *our* championship links!

This course would appeal to men and woman with *real* golfing spirit as opposed to the modern wussies who could freak out at the sight of a wee yellow dandelion near a green or, even worse, suffer a fatal heart attack if they saw a weed on the green itself!

Yet another week later, and we came back again and started on the first and eighth greens with the same procedure as before. We even tried a few rather optimistic putts on the fifth which proved to be a bit premature and a worthless exercise without a hole, and anyway, I never could putt to save myself! This reminds me of the flamboyant Chi Chi Rodrigeuz, who once explained to the press about a very difficult putt that he had one day and his caddie's advice on that very putt. *'He just told me . . . to keep the ball low!'* said Chi Chi. All in all, we were making some excellent progress, and perhaps we weren't completely mad after all.

Then another week elapsed, but this time there was a curious development. Harry had made a visit to Kames golf club, a new golf course in Clydesdale, where he met the architect and business partner of that course, Graham Taylor. Graham had, apparently, been instantly fascinated by what the lunatic brothers had been up to and wanted to know more, much more. So he was duly invited to attend a site visit where all would be revealed. Surely a third patient hadn't escaped the asylum?

So Harry and I walked the entire Roberton course with Graham and reassuringly discovered that we were all singing from the same hymn book. The only difference was that Graham saw a great deal more potential in our little concept than we did ourselves and enquired of us, 'Why go to all this work and effort for just one day and one group? Why don't you think about making a business out of it so that more people can enjoy the experience?'

And that was the spark that ignited our entrepreneurial aspirations and turned everything around. We'd never thought of going the extra mile by entering into the business world. But once Graham's positivity had penetrated into the few brain cells we had between us, we soon became seduced by the possibility of having our very own wee golf course.

A meeting was arranged for the following Thursday evening at Lesmahagow, where Graham's office was located. If we were going to charge people for this experience, then many other factors would have to be taken into consideration in respect of that. Our thinking would have to be a bit more professionally considered, and essentially, much more brainstorming would be required.

We all met as planned and sat and talked for hours about the various possibilities of laying out the Roberton course and how we could make this venture work. As we finished off our brainstorming session, we quite casually informed Graham, 'Of course, there are other defunct courses in the locality to choose from. There's one at Abington too, just along the road from Roberton.'

'Aye,' said Harry. 'And an eighteen holer at Crawford, three at Douglas, and one at Symington, Thankerton, and on the hill at Leadhills!' Both of us had inadvertently become tunnel visioned with Roberton's assets due to the fact that we'd already been scraping and scratching at Roberton's turf.

'Really!' said Graham.

'Oh aye, if you're not doing anything on Saturday, we'll show you round Abington and probably Crawford too, if you have the time? The contours at Abington are really interesting and the turf is ideal for golf.'

'Saturday it is then,' Graham replied.

The response we were getting from Graham was highly satisfying and positive. Even if nothing ever materialised from our meetings, which was always a possibility, this was a good exercise and learning curve for Harry and I.

Saturday arrived and we all met again, this time at the old Abington golf course. Similar to its neighbour at Roberton, Willie Fernie of Troon had laid the course out in 1892. Possibly a double header on the same day for Fernie? Graham instantly took a shine to the place. The course was originally nine holes measuring a meagre 1860 yards, on a fairly compact twenty-five acres of undulating hillside slopes, where drainage was greatly assisted by an extensive network of natural ditches.

The turf at Abington could hardly have been any better for an early inland course. The grass species were mainly fine fescues mixed into a heavy presence of moss, giving it a lovely springy texture to walk upon, and as long as some sheep continued to graze, the sward was kind to the golfer for both finding his ball and playing the ball off the top of it.

We walked the complete course through one to nine, explaining the tee and green locations as we went. Graham had obviously clocked the nearby M74 motorway which links England to Scotland as being a real asset for getting would-be visitors to the course without much difficulty. The motorway is distantly visible from the course, which was deemed as unfortunate from the historical perspective of giving a nineteenth-century experience because of a constant drone on a calm day, but the practicalities of location won the day over Roberton. The natural terrain at Abington would be much easier to maintain than that of Roberton, which had a few acres of almost arable land with predominantly lush grasses within its boundaries. Roberton was more remote, and therefore access for cars would have been really difficult.

Early golf bore no resemblance to the manicured ways of the modern game. In the olden days, a man was a man—and a weed was a weed. When golf was decided upon in any given area, they would generally lay out their course over the winter months when all the natural growth had died back, making it much easier and quicker to start tidying up the land. But before this could happen, a course layout would be required, and during the so-called boom years of the 1890s, the golf course architect came to the fore.

The top professionals of the day found an extra source of income by touring the land at the bequest of towns and villages wanting to engage in this healthy sport, both for themselves and their communities—and the lucrative prospect of the looming massive rise in tourism, courtesy of the railways. Some of the big names included Tom Morris of St Andrews, Willie Fernie from Troon, Willie Dunn Jr and Willie Park Jr, both from Mussellburgh. Going into the twentieth century, the names of James Braid, C. B. MacDonald, and Donald Ross would become synonymous with golf course architecture, which took on a completely different scale and quality from the earlier years. The golf course of the modern twentieth century was—going upmarket!

The considerable upsurge of inventors taking out patents from the 1880s through to the start of the twentieth century was ample evidence as to how much golf was growing internationally as a favoured pastime. These inventors were coming up with all sorts of gadgetry to help golf and its golfers along its evolutionary path. It wasn't only the balls and clubs that were being constantly reinvented, but also hole cups, bags, grass cutting machinery, gloves, indoor golf games, and umbrellas.

The race was on to cash in on this potentially lucrative sporting market. And then there were the literary buffs. Course details were being listed in Golf Annuals, and weekly magazines had begun publishing medal results from all over the United Kingdom as well as the A-Z of all things golf! The great Willie Park Jr published the first book on golf tuition—*The Game of Golf*—in 1896 and was also an inventor of clubs and balls, as well as getting involved in laying out new courses.

Life in general from the mid-nineteenth century up to the 1880s consisted significantly of laborious working hours with little or no leisure time to speak of for the ordinary man. Employers frowned upon any source of sporting recreation as this was regarded as a means of distraction for their employees and an evil deviation from their day-to-day duties. Of course, the privileged few would have their recognised sports in the form of hunting, shooting, fishing, and horse racing—as well as golf!

This was all about to change drastically by the 1890s as people had discovered their own national pastimes of cricket, rowing, football, tennis, athletics, cycling, and golf. Cycling was also important to golf as it became the most popular alternative—other than Shankie's pony—in getting to and from the golf course. In Scotland, there were the additional recreations of quoiting, green bowls, and more especially *the roarin' game* of curling during the long winter months. Now, instead of being resented by the business fraternity, sport was fast becoming an industry within the nation and one which could be exploited through commercialisation.

Football, along with cycling and golf, had dramatically come to the fore with regard to participation sports and their respective commercial opportunities with them. People were flocking to the football grounds in their thousands and paying at the gate for that privilege. Even though football was essentially played by the younger men, anyone could watch as a spectator.

Golf, on the other hand (and contrary to many accounts), was still regarded as an expensive and exclusive pastime, even with the much cheaper gutty balls in circulation! It is true to say that golf did become more affordable to many more people and more accessible due to the vast number of courses being laid out during the 1890s. The fact still remained, however, that the game of golf, in general, was chiefly supported and enjoyed by those who could afford it, sometimes called the *artisans*, and also by those who could find the necessary spare time in which to play it.

One thing which golf did have to offer and remains the same to this day was that it gave all ages of either sex the opportunity to divulge in a marvellous sport and to play it, potentially, for the rest of their natural lives! This evolving sport became a major constituent factor in rejuvenating small towns and villages all over Britain.

Chambers' Journal of 1895 paid this fitting compliment to the game as a result of its growing popularity:

> *There are ports to which, once they have been deserted by the current of commerce, no amount of dock and pier and warehouse building can restore their old importance. In a happy hour some enthusiastic golfer discovers that the land in the neighbourhood of the faded watering-place or the decayed port is admirably adapted to his requirements. A club is formed, the land is rented, local labour is employed in the laying out of the links; the players come down, so do their sisters and wives, and cousins and aunts; houses spring up, the old-world inn blossoms forth as a grand hotel, the local tradesmen have something more to do than to stand sunning themselves at their shop doors—in short, a new flow of life sets in, and the old place once more holds up its head.'*

Again, this was the trend for golf in 1895. But, depending upon the cost of what the club and green fees were, and also the cost of buying clubs and balls, the game would still be out of reach of many would-be golfing enthusiasts in the working classes.

Some things never seem to change as club fees soar each year that passes while the popularity of the game ensures inflated prices in the cost of equipment. The last thing golf needs as we enter a new millennium is its return to what once was predominantly a middle—to upper-class sport! Golf clubs in general could play a much better and more conscientious role by ensuring that the youth of their particular area have *cheap and easy* access to *their* club facilities. On far too many occasions we find that the clubs are doing far too little in this respect, although they often argue the opposite. However, the marvellous Club Golf initiative appears to be ticking all the right boxes.

The actual laying out of a course at the end of the nineteenth century bears no resemblance to the intricate methods applied today by our modern course architects. Messrs Morris, Park, Fernie, or whoever would simply walk the ground in question while surveying and sussing out the possibilities as they went along accompanied by representatives of the club.

Having assessed the ground (preferably from an elevated position), they would proceed to lay out a course based on the professionals' interpretation of the land and how best it could be used for the purposes of golf. They would peg out the tees and greens while quizzing the pros on how to go about the job in hand.

These comments are not designed to detract from the efforts of the early course designers and the valuable work they carried out but merely a deduction of the realities of early golf course architecture. With the advent of the Haskell ball just around the corner in a new century, golf course architecture would take on a significantly different meaning.

Once a course had been mapped out, the actual work entailed in getting a course in order during the 1890s would be undertaken by either an enthusiastic committee or by employing a green-keeper or perhaps a mixture of the two. One of the major costs lay in forming the greens to putt upon, and the area of these, in many cases, would be expected to be no greater than twenty-five square yards per green or thereabouts.

The cheap option for a green was to find areas that could be trained and groomed from what nature already had on offer. If the natural lie of the land didn't accommodate the easy option, then new turf or seeding would be the more costly option. Tees were tees—just level off a small piece of ground and hit it with plenty of sand (Honeyman) and a little seed. No more than a good day's work per tee for a good man. As for the fairways, well, what fairways?

Thereafter, for the next six months or so, the green-keeper would be expected to get his house in order for spring of the following year by continuing to nurture the newly formed greens and tees, while generally tidying up the remainder of the golfing land between tee and green. Thereafter, the course required a healthy membership continually trampling down the longer grasses between tee and green. Thus, the popular saying of the time—*the green will improve with play.*

The other major cost in setting up a golf club was the necessity of having some kind of facility for its members. This sometimes involved the building of a proper clubhouse with toilets, changing room, and lounge area for the more affluent golfers. Others would make do with a glorified shed for shelter and storing their golf clubs in wooden lockers, just as many continue to use today.

It should be noted that all of this investment towards course and premises at the end of the nineteenth century was far from a guaranteed success. The golf craze was still very much in its infancy and the great commercial realities of golf were still to be realised. Setting up a club and golf course in these early days was still a fairly risky business, but the scale of the architecture required help significantly! Prior to the madness of golf's distance boom, a course required much fewer acres, meaning much lower maintenance and leasing costs!

And some, with apparently more brain cells than the Wards, wonder why golf has gotten so bloody expensive again, not to mention the extra time required to walk those extra miles? Still, we're lucky that the *sport* has been in such good hands over the years in order to protect it from turning into just another *game*. Aye, right!

Of course, a golf course is no different today than it was at any time in golf history regarding the unarguable aspect that each and every course is as unique as the other. A typical new course of the 1890s could easily be laid out upon twenty-five to forty acres of land for nine holes. Nowadays, thanks to the distance the new balls can travel that same area which might equate to only three or four holes!

The length of an acceptable bogey four hole would be as little as 250 yards, which gave a drive and short approach shot for the average golfer. When the Haskell ball was invented, around 300 yards would be required for the same drive with a short approach! And that's exactly how golf would evolve for the next hundred years up to the present day, causing havoc as a result! Huh! Progress?

Many other issues arose relating to the lie of the land, including the culling of rabbits and moles due to the extreme damage they caused, and land drains were laid to improve drainage at damp spots. One taboo for these prospective golfers was the presence of any heavy hoofed animals grazing the course. Cattle were totally banned, although horses were often used to help the green-keeper in his duties.

The horses were fitted with specially designed shoes to help prevent them from cutting up the turf so badly. But essentially, after six months or so, you had a perfectly playable golf course, although far from perfect as deemed necessary by the modern tribe. Voila!

Perfect? If there's a pet hate of mine, it has to be the stalwart believer in perfection. It does not exist on this little planet of ours, can't exist, will never exist! Even from the golfing perspective, a hole in one is never a shot of perfect! It's the glorification of one stroke of possible genius by a player, combined with fortuitous elements of nature.

Wind, calm, wet, dry, hot, cold, hard bounce, soft bounce, big fat worm surfaces, and heads ball into hole? Yes, I've been there before and worn that most satisfying T-shirt. And what's more, on the first and only time it ever happened, Harry watched my ball drop into the 18th hole at Biggar on a gorgeous summer's day to give me a tie for first place in the competition!

I knew I had accomplished that magical golfing feat from a distance of 207 yards due to the roar of Harry's voice echoing down the fairway to my hopeful ears. Ya, beauty, I do declare. Even more sweet was the fact that I had satisfactorily struck a clean Max Falkner 3 wood and was partnered by two club champions in Bill Fraser and Dick Thorburn.

The great Ben Hogan reckoned if he could hit six really sweet shots during any round, then he felt he had performed well! Of course, his remaining miss-hits would have been pretty good too as opposed to those of the average hacker.

Bill had one of the finest swings I've ever seen—slow, deliberate, relaxed, rhythmic, a bit like Freddie Couples, only more orthodox than Freddie! He also had a great understanding of the sport and its rules and was often misunderstood for being a stickler for the rules. I often wish I had gotten to know him better and talked more golf with him. Sadly, he's another who has succumbed to that bastard disease—cancer.

Dick, on the other hand, is more of a power golfer. Mostly upper body mechanics—arms, torso and shoulders delivering accuracy of shot after shot from the natural golf department. These highly differing styles of amateur and pro alike prove that *orthodox* is only one way to play good golf! Some people are just so bloody lucky to have a God-given talent when it comes to whacking a golf ball.

Our late friend, Bert Reid, was in the same swing class as Dick but with an amazing snap to his swing. Bert had given up on playing for a few years, but was still highly involved with helping out at the club. Then, for whatever reason, he decided to dig out the clubs and have a game—and he proceeded to break the course record at Biggar!

And then you have the wonderful Irishman, Eamon Darcy, whose swing looked reminiscent of the lumberjack felling trees—but it worked more than ably for him!

If perfection did exist, then golf would be the perfect game to play—but impossible to play perfectly! No, a word of caution for any perfectionists out there. If you're thinking of taking up golf for some fun—DON'T! It will do your brain in! Golf is most definitely *not* a game of perfection. As someone once said wisely—'*perfection is the unattainable goal.*'

Selecting the location for a golf course required several surveys of the local lands that could be available to the golfers, usually through an annual lease with the landowner or tenant farmer. One critical factor lay in the nature of the turf they had before them. The last thing a prospective golfer wanted in the 1890s boom was rich grazing turf more suited for the grazing of livestock.

Generally, the poorer the topography of the grasses, the better it would be for the purposes of golfing all year round! It was not uncommon for some clubs to have a playing season during the winter months only when growth had ceased from September to April if their course was laid out on more lush grasslands or parklands.

The main reason for this was the fact that good grass cutting machinery was still in its evolutionary infancy and a costly expense for any fledgling golf club. The ultimate grass cutters were a flock of sheep for the fairways (what fairways) and a good man with a scythe for the greens! A good scythes man with his razor-sharp scythe could *shave* a green as close as any today!

I have to confess as to doubting the effectiveness of the scythes man until I saw an excellent photograph demonstrating how the greens were cut at St Andrews in the late nineteenth century. Another good reason (although not foreseeable) for laying your new course out on poor, non-arable land would become apparent during the Great War when many courses came under the threat of the plough due to the need to help food production! If a golf course had a few acres of good arable land within its boundaries, then it became a target for the Ministry of Food during those sad and tragic times!

The *Great* War? Hold on; let's put this one to bed! There was absolutely nothing 'great' about the 1914-1918 war! It was more like an indiscriminate assault on the lives of the poor souls who found themselves enwrapped within an organised campaign of genocide masterminded by those who liked their little wars now and again.

This war was nothing more than a shameful slaughter of the innocent masses on *both* sides! The war to end all wars—aye, right! '*Man's inhumanity to man*' as Burns would have said. Some things just never seem to change, lest we forget!

Sunday Golf and the Sabbath Observance

Golf has never been short of controversy throughout its long history, none least when the thorny issue of Sunday golf raised its ugly head, when the sport had taken off in the popularity stakes. The whole issue of Sunday golf would rage on for fifty years!

> *I may not play golf on a Sunday;*
> *Not because it's a sin, it is true,*
> *But simply because Mrs Grundy*
> *Says, 'It isn't the right thing to do.'*

Such was the sentiment displayed by Ronald Ross, a Burgess golf club member in Edinburgh in 1895, when he wrote these words in protest at the opponents of Sunday golf. Never had the sport seen such controversial times since an archer, Patrick Learmont, son of a provost of St Andrews, took a potshot at Archbishop Adamson in 1582 who was *disporting himself 'at the goff' when he should have been preaching!*

The heart of the problem lay in Scotland's strict religious adherence in observing the Sabbath. Feelings, particularly in Scotland, were about to get rather passionate over a period of fifty years and more, in relation to anybody doing anything on the sacred day!

In Europe at the end of the nineteenth century, life was a bit more relaxed as far as the Lord's Day was concerned. Europeans had what was generally called the 'Continental Sunday' which was accepted as the norm there and which was becoming more and more appealing to a British population still living under the strong thumb of the church and their respective congregations.

Scotland's churches, in particular, were dedicated to this Sabbath observance—and some remain so to this day on the western isles! Europeans could freely attend art galleries, museums and the like, play games and sports, and generally, had the freedom to enjoy their Sundays.

Sunday golf *was* played at some of the English clubs and was surprisingly accepted by their relevant communities. The golfers' justification was that the men were tied to work from Monday to Saturday and had little chance of enjoying their game, except that of a Sunday—after sermons, of course, and also with the condition that players carried their own clubs! A little compromise goes a long way.

Meanwhile, back in the hame o' gowf, passions were stirring with various newspaper reports of golfers sneakily breaking the Sabbath by nipping on to trains in Edinburgh and heading south to play on some of the northern English courses which were happy to accept and enjoy their Sunday play! Old Tom Morris had his own views on the subject: *'If the players dinnae need a rest on Sundays, the course does!'*

Somewhat ironically, Scottish ministers had been at the forefront in developing golf into a national pastime by promoting the sport to their congregations. No less than eight ministers joined the Biggar club at its formation in 1895. Golf was seen as being excellent for mind, body, and soul, particularly as many people from the cities were suffering from the effects of an unhealthy industrial revolution.

Smog-ridden cities were affecting the health of the nation, so people were encouraged to take to the open spaces and take in the bracing clean air of the countryside. At the formation of nearly every single golf club in Scotland, you will find the local minister or, ministers, in the first committee of each club. This dedicated association with golfers was going to be tested to the limit because of the growing demand for Sunday golf in future years!

By 1920, many plebiscite votes had been carried out unsuccessfully by various members clubs in support of Sunday golf. The *Dunlop Book of Golf* listed over 600 clubs with only sixteen allowing play on the Sabbath! Golfers in favour of Sunday golf would have to wait until the 1940s before those plebiscites started to turn in favour of golf on a Sunday. As a result, many ministers resigned their memberships in protest.

The ministers within the Clydesdale parishes during the 1890s certainly inherited their predecessors' passion for golf and continued a long line of enthusiasm by providing the inspiration required in getting golf instituted in their respective communities. At Crawford in 1888, the Reverend Christopher McKune laid out a small course of nine holes on his kirk glebe prior to the formation of Crawford golf club in 1890.

We know, from the Lanark minutes, that McKune was a member at Lanark in 1887, but failed to reappear on the members list in subsequent years. Perhaps this was a case of golf espionage, whereby some inside information and experience was necessary before embarking on his own little enterprise of *golf in Crawford*. One thing is certain, he wasted very little time in establishing one of the finest eighteen hole inland golf courses in Scotland, for its time.

In doing so, he also succeeded in surpassing the Lanark clubs' pioneering efforts by creating the district's first eighteen hole course and an impressive first year membership of 200 to support the new venture. It may also be assumed that McKune played his part in having influenced the opening of a railway station for Crawford in the spring of 1891. During the same period, the Reverend Harry L. Dick of Wiston became the first winner of Crawford's Colebrooke Cup and rapidly became a force to be reckoned with, in competitive golf.

It can be assumed that the Reverend Harry Dick was instrumental in the formation of the Roberton club in 1892 and possibly at Abington the same year. He was bestowed the honour of being Roberton's first club captain and promptly secured the record for the green. He replicated the same achievement at Crawford, Abington, and Biggar, which more than justified his *plus* handicap.

Dick was educated at St Andrews University and may well have been the influence in getting Tom Morris down to assist Reverend McKune at Crawford in 1888 to lay out the course and also, perhaps, for getting him to open the Biggar course at Heavyside in 1901.

This ecclesiastical influence upon golf was significant, but at the same time, it had its flaws. Many ministers of the church became the butt of many a joke due to their growing reputation for letting out oaths on poor shots! The following was submitted to *Golf* magazine in 1894:

> *I heard the other day of a Scotsman, a retired minister of the Kirk, who was deploring the tendency of the game to become a ruling passion and also to induce bad language. 'In fact', he said, 'I had to give it up for that reason.'*
>
> *'Give up golf?' exclaimed his friend.*
>
> *'No,' said his reverence, 'the meenistry.'*

All jokes aside, this convivial relationship between the clergy and golf would take a turn for the worse when the plebiscite votes started going in favour of Sunday play. This provoked many a resignation from the men of the cloth who disassociated themselves from their respective club—but not from the sport altogether!

Build It—and the People Will Come!

Building that golf course and trying to set up a business never really concerned me that much. Personally, I never saw it as a massive gamble or a courageously brave thing to do. I'd been self-employed in the building game for over twenty years now, and either it would work or it wouldn't. I've always tended to suss up the worst scenario in moments of life change, and in this particular case it was pretty straightforward, and Harry was there too with his own blend of marketing skills, his ability to source all sorts of tools and materials, and his labour too, as and when it was required.

Essentially, what we required for this wee exercise was a dose of gumption (common sense) and a fair amount of dedicated effort, and after all, nobody was going to die here should something go drastically wrong. Nobody is going to starve to death, are they? What Harry and I desperately needed was some kind of pension plan to see us through to retirement, and this little ploy seemed to fit the bill. Golf, history, and tradition at its best! We weren't getting any younger, and in our line of work, that wasn't getting any easier either. It was like a man once said: *Find a job you like doing, and you'll never work another day in your life.* I was beginning to think that God had a hand in all of this. A fair bit of brainstorming would still have to be done first, though.

We had our vision—a vision of exactly what this course should be and how it should look and play. The entire experience would have to be as authentic as we could possibly make it like the 1890-1910 period in golf history, but there would also have to be compromises and practical solutions for the undertaking. Arbory would be a worthy 'field of dreams!'—a place where the elderly statesmen of golf could come and rekindle nostalgic moments of their past playing days and a place where the young guns of today could get a much needed reality check on the game they play now in comparison to what the sport once was.

Golf had evolved considerably since the likes of Abington had begun their adventure with the sport. We also knew what part we would be playing personally to keep our customers happy and interested throughout the experience. This mission didn't involve rocket science, which was possibly, just as well! We quite simply had to clear up the twenty-five acres before us and make it tidy in the areas where Mrs Nature wasn't very house proud. The biggest problem in trying to tame nature is the way in which she continually undoes any good gardening work as soon as your back is turned.

We had legions of thistles and nettles to contend with; swathes of bracken would creep on to the course from the lower slopes of Arbory Hill, and the rushes were rife throughout the boggy parts of the twenty-five acres and had to be restrained as much as we possibly could.

Rushes are a devil to subdue, as any farmer would tell you. Mole casts littered the place when we first started working on the course which wouldn't have been too bad had the subsoil been earthy rather than full of stones. Stones in the grass would not be conducive to the longevity of the hickory-shafted clubs that we'd have to purchase sometime in the future . . . somehow.

So every single stone had to be lifted and removed from the surface grass. And then, of course, to counterbalance the positivity of having our grass cut for free, we had the sheep shit to clear up! If only we could house-train the buggers to do their business outside the parameters of our golf course how much easier life would be and our backs would be a bit straighter too!

Shit pickin' was a bloody nightmare—not because of the dirty nature of the task, but because it was simply back breaking and an endless chore somewhat in the same lines as it used to be for the painters on the magnificent Forth Railway Bridge—once you got to one side, you went back and started all over again!

I remember some of our first days—taking to the challenge of this thankless chore and my own innocent naivety. The sun was beating down and we were stripped to the waist as we picked away cheerfully to the tones of Rod Stewart and the Corries from the tapes in the car radio. The novelty soon wore off!

I suppose one of the things that helped to inspire us and get our backsides into gear was the fantasy film *Field of Dreams* starring keen golfer Kevin Costner. We recognised similarities in the fantasy of the film to our own dreamy reality. Our field was real in the extreme, and we too could have our famous sporting ghosts, but of a golfing variety in constant attendance, although perhaps not so much in appearance. Build it, and the people will come, Harry. Let's just build it!

Having Graham on board was a confidence booster, and so it wasn't long before we set up a meeting with the Hodge family, who owned and farmed the land of the defunct Abington golf course which sat at the foot of Arbory Hill which is part of Coldchapel farm. Arbory had become the main focus of our attention and the preferred site for the proposed enterprise. Crawford had been seriously considered but was deemed to be too big a venture to undertake as the ground was generally coarser, and anyway, the bloody motorway cuts right through the middle of it now!

Roberton (Ladygill) was very similar to Abington's topography and an excellent candidate, but it was a wee bit remote in location. Douglas too could have been a prime candidate although the Policies nine holer dated from 1922 and was the fourth, and final, location for golf here, and it closed down due to subsidence caused by the coal mines below it!

The first course at Douglas *may* have been as early as 1791 on the Braidley Holms. Many years ago, David Hamilton sent us a copy of a poem from 1791—*On the banks O' Douglas*, which tells of a young student going for a game after lessons, but the contents of the poem are barely conclusive to confirm that it is our Douglas, although we are fairly confident that it is!

No, Arbory would do fine. And getting ahead of ourselves—hell, we could have multi-choice locations in the future for hickory golf once the money started rolling in. As a consequence of selecting Abington as the premier venue, we decided to call ourselves Abington Links Trust.

Speaking of historic Douglas, there was an old story of a local character nicknamed Biff which was narrated to us by the late Jimmy Clarkson. Biff was walking through the grandeur of the estate policies one day and came across the elderly and fragile Earl of Home. As they passed the time of day, Biff became curious. 'Tell me, yer Lordship, how did you come to own all this fine land and Douglas Castle?'

'Oh well, my ancestors fought for all this land hundreds of years ago, and now it's mine,' he replied.

'Really!' said Biff, as he stripped off his jacket and threw it down at the feet of the old gent while starting to spar round the old Earl in boxing fashion.

'What on earth are doing, my man!' he exclaimed.

'C'mon, yer Lordship. Get yer mitts up. I'm going to fight ye for it noo!' challenged Biff.

The proposed fight never took place, and Biff eventually died penniless.

The course at Abington, first laid out by Willie Fernie of Troon in 1892, consisted of nine holes measuring a very modest 1860 yards. The ground was, and still is, a system of beautifully undulating slopes amid a myriad of natural ditches making the entire scene ideal for golf! Ben Sayers, the North Berwick professional, had played the course in 1893, when he said of it, '*I have never seen, for an inland course, such a place so well adapted, so pleasantly situated, and in every way so suited for the purpose.*'

We had already carried out some experimental diggings on a couple of the green locations with the Hodges' full blessing. These trial digs, just as we had done at Roberton, showed us that just a little bit of manicuring to the surface was *not* going to do the job, unlike some of the greens at Roberton where the natural terrain was kind to the making of golf greens!

It became evidently clear to all of us that we were going to have to carry out a helluva lot of work in order to get that little twenty-five acre field back to its original raison d'être! Up until now, the general strategy was to work our way through this new business on a spare time come hobby basis. We were actually having to be careful about this. I, for one, was not a happy chappy with this kind of mentality.

First things first though, we'd have to secure a firm foothold on the ground and a working partnership with the owners. Harry and I had long since made rumblings to the Hodges about the possibilities of restoring the course with a view to setting up a business. This was long before Graham had entered the fray, and everything up till now was very much on an unofficial standing. We knew all the family quite well by now—George and Mary and sons Duncan, George, and Allister. They were all plain-speaking folk and people we could trust without any doubt whatsoever.

Harry and I had been faffing about on the ground in the same way as we had at Roberton, where little intermittent site meetings would transpire with various members of the Hodge family and where thoughts of grandeur were explored. Graham, quite rightly, pointed out that we needed something a bit more concrete in business parlance, and therefore an official meeting with the Hodges was arranged.

Unfortunately, this would inevitably mean talking about a future lease and its cost. So the great triumvirate—no, not Vardon, Braid, and Taylor, but the new triumvirate of Ward, Ward, and Taylor—had a wee private meeting of our own at the 'Welcome Break' services, just over the Clyde from Coldchapel farm and before the upcoming showdown.

As I saw it, we had a couple of potential problems with this meeting. One was Graham and his business acumen and the other was the Hodge's farm manager who was going to be present, obviously touting the cause for the Hodges and justifying his existence. As we sat huddled round our teas and coffee, being aware to keep our voices low and unnoticeable, I took the lead. 'Right, Graham! Now we don't want to be over-complicating this meeting. Just leave the plain speaking to Harry and me, and if we need your expert guidance, we'll just look at you for support.'

'That's fine by me, Alfie. You and Harry know the family better than me,' he replied.

And so we headed over to the farm where the Hodges and their agent were waiting for us. I knew this agent, and he had a bit of a reputation within the farming community for being . . . what shall we say . . . a bit of a stickler. This was going to be very interesting. We all sat down and began to examine the pros and cons from both sides of the fence. From our side, Harry and I initially tried to explain the proposed historical golfing experience and what we needed in order to make this possible.

That quite simply required that we have full access to the ground and permission to make minor excavations here and there to accommodate tees and greens. The other stipulation was that we couldn't have cows grazing on the golf course due to the damage they would cause. And finally, as we didn't have any cash in the kitty, we wanted free access as well, until such times as we could afford it and start trading.

'You want your cake and eat it!' the agent piped in. And to be perfectly honest, he was dead right! And then he continued, as was expected, to reel off the numbers pertaining to the value of the land to the farmer for his grazing, all of which was of no consequence to us, because if we couldn't persuade the Hodges to give this a try with temporary free access, then it wouldn't be happening at all! At this early stage of enterprise, we were considering the prospects of attaining some funding for the project.

Having shown the agent his place, we explained how such an arrangement could be very beneficial to all parties concerned, given a successful outcome and considering that this twenty-five acres was, in farming terms, non-arable and was virtually only useful for sheep, cows, and golfers!

This statement didn't go down too well with the Hodges, but I remembered them from previous conversations we'd had on the course itself when George told me that they'd tried, ever so briefly, to plough the ground. 'We knew it was a waste of time as soon as the plough hit the ground. So we gave it up and never tried again,' George had told us. I also restated my personal opinion, in tactful mode, that it would be highly unlikely that they would ever be allowed to develop this land for housing.

As it stood, our philosophy in starting up a business was that no harm could be done by our presence or by any of our activities on the ground, as we were simply replacing grass with grass. By merely having a gentleman's agreement at this stage in the proceedings bore no real risk, for us, either. I mean, if this little scheme ever came to much, then it would need both Harry and I to see it through.

George and Mary both played golf, and I believe this may have been the deciding factor in allowing us on to the ground. Neither was there likely to be any form of threat from would-be competitors. The meeting ended amicably with Duncan and his father giving a nod of approval and George saying, 'Let's give it a go and see what happens. And we'll get the fencer to erect a twin wire fence along the bottom of the hill to keep the cattle off.'

Excellent! Oh, well. So far, so good! And this is where the real adventure began. Graham, Harry, and I headed off for the Welcome Break and another tête-à-tête with tea and scone before heading for our homes in our own different directions. There would be no stopping us now, and we all displayed great excitement and enthusiasm for our planned venture.

One small pitch for gowf—one giant drive for Abington Links Trust!

The Restoration Begins—For Real

We were now in July 1997, and we rather ambitiously decided to aim for an open day in October of this year and have a trial re-enactment to test the waters. Many notable dignitaries would be invited, including our old pal Sandy Sinclair OBE and past captain of the R&A golf club, and we'd erect a small marquis for the occasion.

Sandy had been a very successful amateur golfer in his heyday and had been very supportive of the Biggar golf club centennial events, and as a result, we'd struck up a good friendship with Sandy. We'd have to get our skates on if this was going to happen at all. All our brainstorming sessions would now be put to the test as we started the venture, for real!

Our earlier concerns with regard to getting the greens properly restored proved accurate because we spent a lot of time trying to level them off, but to no avail!

Another appraisal of the course layout was made with Graham using his golf architectural skills, and any necessary adjustments were agreed. Two holes at the north end of the course, the 4th and 5th, had to be redesigned due to the fact that a house had been built there after the course ceased to operate sometime in the 1930s! The original 4th green was now a garden lawn.

A plethora of tasks had been delegated to each of the new triumvirate. Harry and Graham had a bee in their bonnet with the numerous grassy knolls on the course. Those were described in 1892 as being one of the natural hazards, and I had no wish to see them altered. However, I succumbed and compromised when they suggested we try and level them out where possible, and for this, we acquired the loan of a heavy roadroller from Jim Keith, who was busy getting his new caravan park built only 200 yards from the course.

We brought it up from Jim and tried it on both the fairways (what fairways?) and the 7th and 9th greens. Brilliant! It didn't make a mark on either, although I would have liked to have seen it level off the greens. This was abandoned, but it also highlighted our concerns about getting decent greens resurrected on the cheap. It also highlighted the fact that Mr Keith had a nice wee dumper truck and an old tractor with front bucket and backhoe in his caravan site. Could it be a case for backscratching negotiations as Jim quite clearly needed some help too with his caravan park?

Meanwhile, the big clean-up had begun, and we began scything the new crop of nettles and thistles covering most of the course. You could see the difference instantly, when you turned round and looked at your work. It was most gratifying and a real spur to keep at it whenever we could.

We found four railway sleepers on the course and immediately put them to use by building a small bridge over one of the ditches. Having been quite pleased with ourselves at this achievement, we realised that another forty sleepers would be required for crossings all over the rest of the course. Harry was delegated with the task to find them somehow and sort it out.

The scythe we were using was actually fine for the nettles and thistles, but those bloody rushes were another matter entirely. Harry was delegated the task to organise the loan of a petrol strimmer.

Unfortunately, we still had hundreds, if not thousands, of mole casts littering the entire twenty-five acres, and this would have to be addressed soon. As none of the three of us had the slightest clue about catching moles, I put it to Duncan the first time he was passing, and he assured us that the mole catcher was due to make his annual visit—an elderly man from the Dumfries area.

We would have to make a point of seeing this man and seek his professional advice. The greens were still being tinkered with, but we were making little impression on them. Harry was delegated with the task of getting new greens . . . only kidding. We were going to have to rethink our complete strategy again!

Although we were making good headway, we were already struggling to keep up with Mrs Nature, because a fresh batch of nettles and thistles were reappearing at the places we'd already cut, and as for the bracken at the top of the course, well, we hadn't even touched those areas as yet! There was no way on earth that we were going to be in a position to have people play the course this coming October, especially as we were only working at the course part-time! And those bloody moles were laughing at us.

Just as Duncan had told us, the old mole catcher appeared one day, and we spoke to him as he was about to do his business on the golf course. We had a wee natter about this and that and how we were trying to restore this field back to a golf course. All this time he had obviously clocked that we were both dirty smokers.

'So, we cannae wait for you to come every year to clean this place up. How dae ye catch moles?' I asked.

The mole catcher didn't look too keen on revealing his trade secrets to us and just said, 'Ach. Nane o' the twa o' ye will ever catch a mole in yer lives, son! Yer baith smokers and they'll smell ye a mile awa'!' And that was the extent of his advice as he made his way on to the course to set his first trap.

We were both a bit put out with his disinterest in trying to help us, and Harry asked me, 'Aye. What are ye going to do now, then?'

'Simple. We're going to go and watch what the auld bugger does. Can't be rocket science, can it?' I replied.

We followed him on to the course, making up some chat as we went and saying that we were heading up the hill to check out some work we'd been doing there. Bloody liar! The mole catcher came to what looked like a freshly dug cast of earth and levelled it off with his hand and then poked around for something. Hmmm. This was interesting.

It was actually the wee hole that the mole creates while digging like the wee bugger that it is! He then took his miniature spade off his shoulder and dug out a square of turf the approximate size of the trap at this hole and then cleared out the loose earth or stones. He was looking for the underground run that the moles use, and thereafter, he simply placed the half round spring trap in the same direction as the run.

Then he just placed the sod of turf on top of the trap so as not to foul it from springing the trap and drove a small peg into the ground near the trap as a marker for going back to retrieve the trap later that day—hopefully with a wee mole stuck in it!

'Oh well. We'll leave you to it. Maybe see ye next year, eh?' I said as Harry and I walked away. Once a good twenty yards up the hill, I said to Harry, 'There. Ah told ye, it's no rocket science. All we need is for you to get some mole traps!'

Harry thought for minute and said, 'I wonder if they've got any at the farm?'

Moles can cause an immense amount of damage to the land as can be witnessed when you look at a badly infested field. Bad enough for Mr Farmer, but intolerable for a green-keeper! We decided to ask Duncan or George if they had any traps of their own the next time we saw one of them and hopefully try this mole-catching lark for ourselves.

There were going to be loads of problems to overcome in this venture before we were finished, that was for sure, but I've always lived by the theory that you only have a problem if you can't find the solution for it! With regard to the moles, we had the solution; we just had to learn how to administer it.

A few days later, we saw George, and he confirmed that there were a few traps over at Craighead farm and we could take them if we wanted them. We did and duly found them in an outbuilding and brought them back over to the course. The mole catcher had done his job well and apparently caught about forty of the little blighters on Arbory's slopes.

However, we all knew that they hadn't been eradicated altogether, and new ones would find their way on to the ground from the surrounding lands, and therefore a constant lookout would be necessary to keep on top of the situation providing, of course, that Harry and I could do the job ourselves. Time and a little experience would tell.

Meanwhile, we could now begin to clear up the hundreds of unsightly mole casts littering the entire course. A major time-consuming task that would require some assistance from a team of juvenile enthusiasts already earmarked for the job—my son, Ross, and some of his pals.

All kinds of things were being sorted out as we continued on our quest. Graham was busy setting out prices for various packages and drafting promotional stuff for leaflets and advertising as well as trying to sort out a scorecard and presenting various cash flow projections. As far as the scorecard was concerned, we had agreed to name most of the holes after the names of the surrounding hills.

No 1. Arbory 198yds; 2. Coldchapel 318yds (after the farm); 3. Tintock 264yds (the old name for Tinto); 4. Craighead 102yds; 5. Southwood 188yds; 6. Ravengill 130yds; 7. The Road 233yds (at the bequest of Harry); 8. Priestgill 186yds; 9. Fernie's 239yds (after the course designer) Total yardage; 1858 yards. These yardages compared very favourably with the original layout which was stated at 1880 yards.

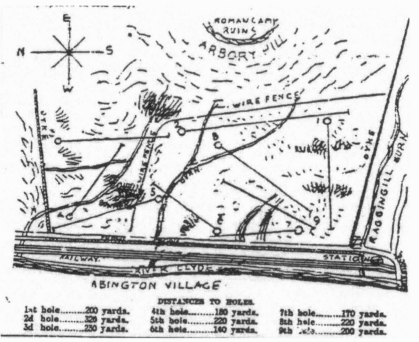

Original Sketch of Abington Golf Course, 1892.

We were also having to think of all the administration details, possible planning permission, rates liability, the lease on the ground, setting up a bank account, legal and accountancy fees, stationary items like fee tickets and receipts, public liability insurance, signage, course accessories like flags, hole cups and pins, and loads more!

Inevitably, the raising of all these cost factors opened up a massive can of worms relating to financial projections! Anything Harry and I had done in the past had been done on the cheap which involved a strategy of beg, steal, or borrow. Although the old and trusty strategy would still apply to many of our overheads, the reality became clear that we were going to have to pay for something. And that was going to be a real problem for two working-class bankrupts!

We all muddled our way through 1997 where our over-ambitious plans for a trial run in October were abandoned. Everything else regarding the project remained 'on board' with the three of us still fully committed to seeing this through. Alas, we were going to have to rethink our strategy once more, and meetings continued periodically through the winter months and little was done on the course! All this dilly-dallying had me wondering why we couldn't get this damned business up and running in a matter of months, like they did a hundred years ago.

However, there was a small development on my side of the fence when my mother-in-law phoned my wife Dorothy one night, at the end of August, to tell us that she had won the lottery! Bloody hell! To say my head was full of mince at this time would be a total understatement! Day-to-day work on the building site had long since become a real drag on my emotions due to the Arbory project merely lingering in the background, while I desperately wanted Arbory to be at the forefront in my list of active priorities!

The main family consisted of two brothers and two sisters, of which one was my wife! Surely, I thought, there would be a handsome payout heading our way, and if so, it was going to change everything.

We had another meeting in September 1997 to try and iron out the solution for getting the greens in order. We'd also finally agreed that the only way we were ever going to achieve good greens was by scraping and re-turfing the entire nine greens! This meant incurring considerable expense, but we were committed and united in our opinions that it had to be done.

The latest suggestion came from Graham, whereby we would be able to acquire turf by using the Kames golf course turf cutter and re-lay all of the nine greens. The only problem with this was that we needed about 900 square yards of fairly decent turf that was accessible and cheap.

First port of call for this was the local bowling club in Abington who, we had heard, had secured a healthy grant to lay a completely new green and build a new clubhouse for its members, probably about forty to fifty members in total. Oh well, good on them and good funding if you can get it. I don't grudge any community project which has the savvy to plunder the public funding barrels. However, sometimes more affluent communities can well afford to dip into their own pockets like Biggar did in 1907 to create the public park and golf course.

They also had two old Portakabins that they could sell to us, so we headed over to inspect the existing green and the kabins. We were told that the kabins were available to us for £300 if we transported them back over to the course ourselves, but the existing green was apparently designated to another home.

Personally, I felt a bit miffed at a small group getting tens of thousands in grant funding, then having the cheek to ask us for £300 for kabins that they probably had to get rid of anyway. As it was, we needed them, and nobody was funding a new clubhouse for 'hickory golf'! We needed some form of shelter for ourselves and somewhere to store our tools. Looking back now, and as I write, I'm thinking they could have given us a wee break with those kabins.

We were learning some basic laws of enterprise. We were also learning so much from the land and Mother Nature on our mission, none less in respect of the fact that the hill was totally infested by rabbits. Now, by this time, we had almost mastered the art of mole catching. All we did, because we were both dirty smokers, was to copy the actions of the old mole catcher, but we had to make sure our nicotine-stained hands were insulated with surgical gloves and then a pair of heavy duty gloves on top of them! It seemed to do the trick nicely because we were nipping the little buggers as soon as they reappeared by digging fresh casts. There was one humorous occasion where we extracted a trap from the ground to find two wee hairy bums extruding from either side of the trap. A doubler no less—awww! Rabbits, however, would prove to be a different kettle of . . . well, rabbits.

Those pesky rabbits would prove to be a real thorn in our sides! I remember a mate, Scott Jamieson, who once worked with the forestry, planting trees, telling me about his version of the nice wee bunny rabbits. 'The wee bastards just nip the buds aff the top of the trees, and that's enough to kill them. They don't even eat the buds. They jeest dae it fur spite!' he would tell me.

I used to laugh about this summary of the rabbit, but it proved to be perfectly accurate when Allister from the farm dropped off a bundle of spare trees left over from a tree planting exercise elsewhere. I didn't have any protectors but decided it would be OK for Harry and myself to plant them on the course away from the field of play and get them protected from the rabbits later. Bad decision! Within two days, I noticed that every bloody tree, about forty in all, had a wee slither of bud sitting at the base of each tree. Total waste of time, and they were digging holes on the course too! Scott was right. This was war!

There were a couple of guys who had the shooting rights over the grounds of the course and Arbory Hill. But these guys weren't interested in total extermination of the wee furry creatures because that would eliminate their need to be there at all! They were happy to get a day's shoot now and again full in the knowledge that the little hairy buggers who escaped the buckshot would be busy making new hairy buggers to reinstate the population figures!

We came to the conclusion that we would have to set up our own defences against the enemy. As we didn't have a gun at our disposal and neither of us was a crack shot, we decided to visit the ironmongers in Biggar and invest in a few wire snares. This would be yet another learning curve for Ward bros and one which would cause a bit of a stir.

We bought ten brass wire snares and took them on to the course and tried to set them at the trouble spots—with murderous intent. We didn't have a bloody clue as to what we were doing and just made up our own rules as we went along. Unlike the rabbits, our actions were not borne out of spite. All we were trying to do was to protect our wee bit of Scotland, which wanted to be a golf course.

With the deed done, we retired for refreshments and to focus our efforts on some of the other numerous tasks in hand. We kept checking the snares for a couple of days with no signs of any success until the neighbour from the top end of the course came in bleating that there was a rabbit caught in a snare in the middle of the course. 'We'd better go up and see what he's gibberin' about,' said Harry.

So we walked up the seventh fairway (what fairway?) to the centre of the course, and the squeals started to penetrate the eardrums. The little bugger wasn't difficult to find, and when we got next to it, we could see that we'd managed to 'foul' snare the rabbit. Somehow, only its paw was caught in the snare, and the pair wee thing was squirming about aimlessly. I looked at Harry and said, 'Well, what are you waiting for? Get on wi' it!

He looked back somewhat puzzled and asked, 'Get on wi' what?'

'What do ye think? Ye'll have to kill it—rabbit stew!'

'Bugger off—ah'm no killin' it,' he said defiantly. A short debate ensued with a stalemate outcome. He wasn't going to do the business, and I certainly wasn't going to do it either. When it comes down to killing anything in cold blood, I just don't have the stomach for it, and neither did Harry. The little bastard was released and sped off without having the decency to feign a limp!

The incident was reported to Duncan by the 'Good Lifer', and we were asked to lift all the snares we had laid. Personally, I can't abide cruelty of any kind, but this was a case of survival of the fittest. I also knew that we would be pulling our hair out with the damage these pesky little critters kept causing on the course and could only hope that the shooters didn't stay away too long between visits. For whatever reason, perhaps spite, they continued to scrape and burrow all over the course which would be even worse once we eventually got the greens sorted out. Buggers!

I did get the last laugh with the neighbour at the end of the course though. When I was up there working on the fifth tee, I noticed they had a mole in their garden and it had just begun making a cast on their pretty lawn. I'd become quite proficient at catching the buggers, so I shouted over the fence to them and said, 'Hello, I see you've got a mole there. If you want, I'll bring up some traps the next time I'm up here and catch it for you.'

Mrs Good Life panicked immediately and told me, 'Oh no! Just leave it alone. It has as much right to be there, as we have.' I acknowledged her request with a wave of my arm and turned away laughing.

A couple of days later I was passing by and couldn't help but notice the array of mole casts all over their lawn and the two of them trying to tidy up the mess. I never said a word, but I knew full well that if Mr Mole set foot on *our* ground, only a few feet away—he was dead meat!

The Joys of Gutta-percha

By September of 1997, we had all agreed that we really needed new greens of some description, and it was obvious that completion of the project was still a long way from being a sellable experience. Added to that, we still didn't have a source for either buying or making period gutta balls. This was discussed at another meeting at Kames golf club where, after giving Graham some basic details on gutta-percha, he decided to get on the phone and see if he could come up with anything.

After only half an hour, Graham re-entered the Kames lounge in an exuberant mood and clearly very excited. He had phoned a rubber company in Aberdeen who put him on to a company in London, where he won his eureka moment, both for himself and the project!

Silvertown, United Kingdom, was once one of the largest golf ball manufacturers at the end of the twentieth century and produced a highly popular ball—the 'Silvertown'. Although no longer making golf balls, they told Graham that they could supply 'purified' gutta-percha offcuts from their manufacturing process if we needed them and that a sample was on its way! This tremendous breakthrough earned Graham many brownie points and took the edge off the ongoing problems and disappointments with getting those bloody greens in order.

A couple of days later, Harry appeared at my door at about nine in the evening, all excited. He had been summoned to Graham's office in Lesmahagow earlier in the evening where Graham gave him the gutta samples that had arrived that day.

'C'mon then,' I demanded, 'let's see what this stuff looks like.'

He opened the package, and there before our eyes was a small lump of black gutta, probably enough to make two or three balls. We quizzically inspected the sample and had a good sniff at it. Yes, it did have a rubbery odour to it.

Harry looked at me and said, 'What now?'

'Well! I'm buggered if I know why the two of you didn't get busy and boil the bloody stuff up yourselves.'

'Och. We thought you'd better see it first. We didnae want to upset ye,' he said.

'Silly buggers. So what do you think we should do with it?' I asked Harry.

Harry pondered before mumbling, 'Shouldn't we wait until Graham's here too?'

'Nah! Let's get on wi' it. I'll need to find an old pot to boil it up in. What do you think? He who hesitates is lost. Eh?'

It didn't take a great deal of time or persuasion for Harry to agree with me, and so we began our own historic golf ball making process. The gutta began to soften in the boiling water as we poked and prodded at it with a fork. Now, Archie's Willie Park 'Bramble' mould had been lying about the house for a couple of months getting dusty. This mould hadn't seen gutta-percha for over a hundred years, and now it was making its own historical comeback!

We took the softened gutta from the pot and cut off a piece which we thought would be appropriate to fill the mould. It was hand-rolled to a nearly round sphere and placed into the mould. Who knows, maybe Willie Park Jr had handled this very mould himself? I had already purchased a G clamp to use as a press for squeezing the mould, and the pressure was applied and left for a minute or two to cool down.

Everything we were doing was very much out of blind ignorance as we'd never came across any specific details in our research as to how to properly mould a golf ball. But we would learn as we went along. This was *our* prototype, and it was ready to be removed from the mould whether it was ready or not, such was our impatience.

When we took it out, it became obvious that we'd used just a little too much gutta because it certainly wasn't round, more obese than it should be. There was also a heavy 'fin' round its circumference, which was cut off with a sharp craft knife. It was still warm and slightly soft, so we popped it into the freezer for rapid hardening and had a fag while it cooled down.

We thought it might be a good idea to open all the doors and windows of the kitchen, because this stuff was a wee bit pongy too! What fun this was! And the childish exchanges of 'patter' were quite acceptable—at least it was for Harry and me.

When we retrieved the ball from the freezer, it had certainly cooled to a much firmer state, but something wasn't quite right. There was a simple test. If it didn't float, it wasn't the right stuff. All prior excitement was short-lived, because the bloody thing sank like a brick in the pot full of water! The problem was that this gutta had been purified, and what we required was gutta straight from the tree with all its impurities still intact. Back to the drawing board.

Graham was asked to get back in touch with Silvertown and ask if they had any other types of gutta they could sell us. They had, and it was much cheaper than the black gutta sample already received! They duly sent another sample to Graham, and it was delivered to us in a matter of days. They had told Graham that there were blocks of old gutta that had been lying in a corner of the factory for as long as anyone could remember.

This time the gutta was brown in colour, and before we started to boil it up, to soften it, we put it in a large pot full of water to see if it would float. Thankfully, it did float, and we set about making gutta balls for real. Like everything else put before us, we became very proficient at making good quality guttas which were fully compliant and authentic to the original balls made from 1848-1870s. This was a massive step in the right direction for the hickory experience!

From the 1870s, people were pioneering various attempts at making composite balls using gutta as a cover to encase other materials like rubber, cork, metal filings, etc. This era of the ball is generally termed the 'gutty' era to distinguish it from the 'pure' guttas made previously. Strangely, rubber had been a known material as early as 1736 and balls were definitely being made from it—but for some reason or another not golf balls. The American Indians had been using rubber to make balls for their games as early as the eleventh century!

Due to the decimation of the gutta plantations to satisfy demand, gutta became more difficult to source, and rubber then became the main material for making golf balls. When Coburn Haskell invented his rubber wound balls in 1898, the game of golf would never be the same again.

The performance of all the different balls varied immensely. The feathery was soft and must have been a pure delight to play with constantly, whereas the guttas felt like you were hitting a small rock but gave off the famous 'click' when struck well. I believe the feathery and the first gutta balls were equidistant in length, probably in the 150-180 yard range for a good drive.

Willie Park Jr stated 200 yards to be a long drive with a gutty during the 1890s era. And then along came that Haskell with its rubber wound interior and softer feel, which was much easier to get airborne and sprung off the face of the club—and the special bonus was at least twenty more yards off the tee!

Commonly known as *the bounding Billy*, this ball would bounce and roll more readily than its predecessors and therefore yield more distance for each shot. As a result, golf courses began to shrink in *scale* because of the new ball!

Personally, I think the innovation of the Haskell was a fantastic development for golf and golfers, but this is the point where lessons should have been learnt with regard to the ball getting out of hand in relation to invention and further improvements. Golf was beginning to lose some of its challenge, and certain elements of skill were being lost too.

For the first time in golf's history, an improvement to the ball had shown just how much it could affect the design and architecture of a golf course, especially the 1,500 new golf courses, which had been laid out to suit the gutty ball from 1890 to 1900! The *balance* and *scale* of the ball's performance in relation to the golf course was now being highlighted and questioned by a few astute golf writers at this time. Alas, nobody took any notice of these protagonists, and here we are, a century later, and nobody takes any notice of the modern protagonists either. *Protect and preserve?* I don't think so!

One of the leading protagonists highlighting the changes happening within golf from 1900 to 1930 was a prolific golf writer by the name of Max Behr. Behr was an accomplished American amateur golfer, whose writings on the sport are not so widely known outside of his native America. He became a recognised golf course architect, designing courses through the 1920s, but before this career move, he was made the editor of *Golf Illustrated* in 1914.

It was through this new job as editor of one of America's first golf magazines that Behr found the ideal platform to publish his views and opinions of the greatest sport the world has ever known. His editorials covered every aspect of golf in academic fashion, almost cryptic, making the reading of his work quite hard going at times—especially for *dunderheids* such as myself.

But more of Behr later, because I hadn't quite found him yet, in relation to this book!

In regard to our hickory project, we all recognised that that we had a problem with the ball, something that the ruling bodies have failed to confront for a mere century now! In our case, we didn't have a suitable ball which would complement the proposed historical experience. That little problem was now fully resolved by finding the elusive gutta-percha.

Modern golf on the other hand has a slightly more serious problem due to the fact that those ruling bodies do not recognise any problem at all with *their* ball.

The Importance of Golf

As another winter was beginning to set in, we spent the next few months doing everything, except getting the greens in order. Graham and I tried to find some proof of feasibility for the project by comparing various cash flow projections. Finding the facts hard to bear, I had to concede with Graham's figures that we were struggling to make the numbers stack up. Bugger!

What's more, we were still looking for that elusive turf that we could cut and re-lay ourselves, but nothing ever became available. As a consequence, we agreed that a new and realistic target date for starting to trade would be spring 1999. I was losing the will to live!

We all continued with the day jobs and saw the winter out. It wasn't all bad though, because my wife, Dorothy, had received the anticipated windfall from her mother's lottery win. We were more financially secure than we had ever known, but by the time our debts were cleared, a decent second-hand car purchased, and the council house we were living in was purchased, those welcome funds had sustained a considerable dent!

Having said that, it was bloody marvellous to be free from money concerns, and it also allowed me the luxury of not having to work full-time and flat out in the building game, at least for now.

After a lengthy layoff, we reconvened at Harry's house in April 1998 and had a meeting to decide where our futures lay and that of Abington Links Trust. The outcome was encouraging as all three of us confirmed our commitment to stay with it, and Graham stated that he'd made enquiries about buying reject turf for those bloody greens.

We didn't need the high-quality stuff that the new courses were using. If it was green in colour and cheap, it would do the job fine.

There was even talk of trying to secure leases on other historical golf sites in the district—places like Roberton, Crawford, Douglas, and Leadhills where golf had been played and then abandoned in the past.

We may have been getting ahead of ourselves, but it was much better to be in a positive state of mind. At the same meeting, we decided to try and pursue funding from the R&A and local enterprise agencies while Harry would begin his campaign of promoting and marketing the experience.

This must have been a time of high spirits for all concerned because we were seriously getting our house in order. Potential helpers for scraping out the greens were considered but not required when Duncan offered to have them scraped off for us by using his own JCB digger machine complete with an able driver. Not only that, he agreed to waive any fee due for the lease on the ground, due to our inability to pay it! The moles were infesting the ground again and the ditches were in need of being cleaned, but we thought we shouldn't push our luck with Duncan and left those matters for another day.

True to his word and only a week later, Duncan sent his digger and driver, Sam Elder, to commence work on the course. Harry and I had already lined all the nine greens with marker paint, and we would oversee the work as it progressed. All the scrapings from the greens would be utilised to make teeing areas in close proximity to each new green.

Each green took about one hour to scrape and then shift the scrapings and level them off for the new tees. Sam was a great wee guy, and nothing we suggested to him was too much bother—just the kind of person you like working with. We now had a golf course in the making!

All this positivity was getting too much for me to handle considering all the uncertainties of the past two years. Progress was in lift-off mode because Duncan himself suggested that we should clean the ditches out as, from a farming perspective, they were in need of being done anyway. Holy shit! The twin wire fence that George had promised to have erected on the boundary of the course and Arbory Hill to keep the cows off the course was scheduled for erection in a week's time! This was a marvellous spell we were having.

Sam appeared daily for several days to clean out the ditches which, in some ways, were causing a bit of a mess. There would be a lot of manual landscaping required to get the ditches look green again, but it was all a necessary part of the restoration process. These same ditches would be hand-dug before machinery made the task so much easier. All this digging and shifting of turf had put another idea into Harry's head. He suggested that we could form a couple of small ponds by damming up the ditch with some of the turf scrapings.

As an initial thought, I totally rubbished the suggestion on the grounds that we would be drifting away from the authenticity of the original course—there weren't any ponds in 1892, so why should we create them now? He was determined to win me over and argued that they would look terrific and enhance what was, generally, a rather bland landscape as there were no bunkers.

Added to this argument, he suggested that the ponds could be a valuable source for fresh water. That was an excellent point and won the day for me. Sam was instructed to dam up the ditch to form a couple of ponds, which would now feature at the fourth and eighth holes. Compromise is wonderful, and he is my brother after all!

By mid-May, we had decided to form a limited company with Harry, Graham, and myself as directors, and hopefully, we'd coax Duncan into becoming more involved with the project by becoming a director too. The Hodges had been fantastic landlords to date by investing plant, machinery, and time as well as having the twin wire fence erected at their own expense. Asking Duncan to accept a directorship of this new company seemed the right and natural thing to do. When the suggestion was first put to Duncan, he appeared quite keen on the idea but didn't commit outright.

The new company would be given the grand title of World Heritage Golf Links Ltd, and Graham would start the process of forming the company through his own lawyers. Meanwhile, the topsoil was being ordered to replenish the nine locations of the greens. We would need at least 100 tons and had nowhere to stock the topsoil on the course itself, so Duncan agreed to have it dumped at nearby Coldchapel farm.

All the digging work on the ditches was now complete, and it was now up to ourselves to start getting everything back to a more eye-warming scene because the whole course was looking rather rugged and haggard. All the ditches, although now running clean and free, badly needed landscaping, and worst of all, the scrapings were full of stones and boulders. The boulders we could use for crossing point foundations and backing up the dams created to form the two ponds, hence the old adage: *Use what you've got, and you'll never be without!*

One of our restoration problems was trying to find ways of accessing the entire course for either Jimmy's dumper truck or our own cars. More railway sleeper bridges would be built as and when we could muster up another four or five sleepers for each bridge.

I had taken delivery of the fore-mentioned topsoil and saw it dumped at the farm as agreed by Duncan. The only problem was that I had inadvertently dumped it at the wrong place. Oh dear, I've buggered up again! Actually, it worked out quite well because we wanted it transported back on to the course as soon as possible so that we could start work on the greens whether by seeding of re-turfing. Duncan wasn't too chuffed with yours sincerely and actually told me, 'It's nae use there. Ah need it shifted right away, Alfie.'

Oh dear, this was a terrible mistake for me to make. I thought I'd better make some form of phoney apology: 'I'm really sorry, Duncan, but I thought it would be all right where it was and out of your way. I suppose you'll be getting it up on to the course quite soon then?'

He looked at me and grumped, 'Aye. Ah suppose so, ya bugger. Ah'll need to do it at nights because we're busy wi' other things on the farm the noo.'

All's well that ends well. Ya beauty!

Harry and Graham were busy with all sorts of admin stuff, including drafting the scorecard and leaflets and arranging the printing of the same. They had also taken a wee trip up to the old defunct Muirsland course at Lesmahagow, where the old gang mowers were lying rusting away. They had spoken with Mrs Barr, the farmer's wife, who had given consent to have them removed. Such items could be used on the course as green-keeping relics of the past. Grass rollers had also been secured courtesy of the farmer, Mr Griffiths, at the nearby Meadowhead course at Roberton.

Early green-keeping practices, especially on inland courses where the grasses were lusher than those of the seaside links, favoured the practice of heavy rolling of the grass. As techniques, experience, and gang mowers evolved, this practice was deemed unfavourable in later years, due to the severe compaction of the sward, and this rolling caused far more damage to the grass than any good it was doing by trying to create fairways.

I was kept more than busy at the course, trying my best to level off and landscape the ditch areas as well as dig out new drains here and there. Harry would appear most nights or during the day if his work brought him to the area. I was also starting to drain some of my wife's windfall because I wasn't earning a great deal from the building trade at this time. I suppose I was being rather selfish by neglecting the need to keep some cash coming in, but I felt the course was now top priority, and hopefully, any shortfalls at home could be rectified at a later date.

We had another meeting with George and Duncan Hodge, where Duncan verbally agreed to become an equal partner in the business with Harry, Graham, and myself. More importantly, Jim, the farm labourer, had been instructed to start carting the topsoil to the greens. All parts of the course were accessible by a tractor with the exception of the area at the third green. This area of the course was practically cut off by the ditches because of the boggy nature of the land.

We were going to have a serious issue with access to the third green for quite a while until such times as we could get good crossing points organised. The last thing we wanted just now was a tractor churning up swathes of the course which would, obviously, have to be repaired and made good!

The calendar told us we were now in the middle of July, and it brought our first funding appeal knock back, courtesy of the Royal and Ancient at St Andrews. The blazers were surprisingly unimpressed by our historical efforts, and their somewhat curt and unsympathetic rejection left all three of us even less impressed by their total ignorance in the handling of the matter! *There could be trouble ahead . . .* Oh, the rascals!

They were busy sending millions abroad in an effort to globalise the sport but couldn't keep a few coppers in the 'hame' itself to help promote a unique business with golf's history and traditions firmly at heart. And not a simple *good luck anyway* to finish off their . . . note! Oh, the rascals!

Time to move on. So we put the R&A and their blazers on the 'not worth a shit' pile and tried to forget the disappointment. It became blatantly obvious that we would have to raise funds from somewhere to keep the dream rolling along. Harry and Graham chased up various ways of securing sponsorships and essential funding, as bills would have to be paid for turf and perhaps reproduction sets of hickory clubs.

Enquiries had been made to Barry Kerr and Hamish Steedman at St Andrews, where their company made repro hickory clubs. We had two options for supplying clubs for our customers. We could buy old playable antique hickories through dealers or auctions and make up sets of our own. That is to say, we could collate bags of clubs made up of various clubs from different club makers because the early golfer didn't have a *matched* set of clubs.

Or we could purchase the more expensive repros from Heritage Golf. The latter of the options meant that everybody who played at Arbory would be using the exact same equipment. There could be no excuses from the golfers that 'your clubs are better than mine'.

The famous 'Nicoll of Leven' clubmaker dating back to 1881 was the first company to produce *matched* sets of irons in 1926. Heritage Golf was producing the Gem brand which was highly popular amongst golfers in the 1920s. Each set consisted of Brassie (2 wood), Midiron (3 iron), Mashie (5 iron), Mashie Niblick (7 iron), Niblick (9 iron), and putter.

They also made a Mashie Cleek which was a driving iron, but we decided to cut our costs and leave this one out of the bag, the reason being that most players would struggle with the equivalent of a one iron, and as the great Lee Trevino would advise, '*If you ever get caught in a lightning storm hold up your one iron and point it at the sky, 'cause even God can't hit a one iron!*' Trevino was an ever cheerful character on the course and was one of the finest ever exponents of one iron play . . . and yes, he was struck by lightning!

I know that millions would echo my following statement, but my mother was the best! Not only did she raise all of us with very meagre earnings from Dad's hard working efforts, but she possessed a hidden talent for art and poetic prose, a quality that Pat and Grace would inherit from her genes.

She was also a terrific cook, seamstress, and had hands that were prepared to tackle almost every task presented to them. And then there was her unstinting belief in Christianity and God, not in religion, because she was never a church goer . . . thankfully! I think there was too much hypocrisy from within the Lord's house for her liking.

Dad was a quiet and unassuming man who kept himself to himself as a rule. He'd been in the thick of some of the fiercest action during the war in the North Africa campaign and up through Sicily and into Italy. I think I only ever saw him in his underpants once when I was only a boy, but the sight left me with an unforgettable image. The whole of his left side was spattered with shrapnel wounds, and we all knew that the subject of dad's involvement in the war was a taboo area.

Mum would tell us, like so many mothers would tell their children, *'Your dad was never the same man when he came back from the war. Those who saw the worst of it will never talk about it!'* On the funnier side, he always enjoyed a few whiskys at New Year when you'd hear his heartfelt rendition of Burn's *'My love is like a red, red rose'*, audibly massacred with his half brummie and half Scottish accent.

Mum fell ill at the end of summer 1998 and was admitted to our local 'Kello' hospital in Biggar. The doctor diagnosed her problem as being that of old age.

She was eighty-six and never knew an idle bone in her wracked body. 'Your body is tired out, Mrs Ward,' the doctor told her. All of the family had never seen so much of each other in years as we did then, when we all visited the hospital regularly over several weeks. In the end, she just 'let go' of life as I gently held her hand, and she passed away peacefully on the Sunday morning of 18 October 1998.

Ae fond kiss, and then we sever,
Ae fareweel, alas forever . . .'

Tourism, Revenge, and Twa' Puddocks!

Life goes on—apparently.

Eight greens had been prepared and awaited the arrival of a lorry load of turf from York in England. The third green remained a problem with access. Graham had successfully negotiated 1,000 square metres of good quality sports turf at a bargain basement price of just £1.50 p per square metre. Still we'd have to find 1,500 quid between us though.

When the turf arrived, the lorry was too long to get over the tight ninety-degree turn at the railway bridge, and we were forced to have it dumped near the old station on the other side of the Clyde. This would require another favour from our friendly farmer. Graham was keen to have a look at our purchase, and he was clearly delighted by the quality considering the turf was supposed to be reject quality.

Thankfully, Duncan came to the fore once more, and Allister, his brother, brought most of it up to the course about a mile distant. We recruited some able assistance from Tam Lammie from the village, and between Harry, Tam, and myself, we had five greens laid on the first day and night! Each green was ring-fenced with temporary plastic fencing to protect them from the marauding sheep in the meantime. There could be no turning back now!

Eventually, we intended to leave the greens open without erecting permanent low fences as had been common when the sheep normally grazed a course and can still be found on a few courses, like lovely Brora in the Highlands. Harry and I can both remember what a pain in the backside these fences were at Biggar when we first took up the game.

The remaining greens would be laid over the next week due to the diabolical weather we had been experiencing, but the third was proving a right pain. We just couldn't get close to it at all. An attempt had been made to get the tractor over the ditch, but the ground was simply too boggy; the tractor was making one helluva mess and could have got stuck completely!

There was a bonus though. We weren't sure how far the turf would go in getting the greens covered, but it turned out that we probably had enough left over to cover the nine tees as well! Reluctantly, we decided to roll out the turf designated for that third bloody green as it would perish if it was left rolled up.

The small matter of planning consent cropped up, and it was decided to get in touch with the local planning department as a precaution against disaster. There was the two Portakabins to think about, but the course itself could be considered as being existing, wouldn't it? We all know what planners can be like and the authority they like to administer.

Everything was now advancing at breakneck speed. The greens were all laid with the exception of the third, and most of the new tees had also been turfed. It was November and all growth was in retreat, giving us respite from the thistles, nettles, and rushes, which in turn allowed us to concentrate on some fun elements of making the place look like a golf course.

Harry was busy strimming pathways through the deep hazardous rushes, which gave both a sense of direction to the golfer and a pleasing look to the eye. Most of the barren areas which had been scraped were now landscaped and seed sewn to restore some greenery.

Negotiations were ongoing with Barry and Hamish at St Andrews to secure sets of hickory clubs, and at the same time, he informed us of a similar project at Oakhurst Links in America. Two months had elapsed since Mum died, and being so busy at Arbory had taken our minds off that sad loss. But, when needed, we could both pick our own times for silent reflection upon this wonderful space we had.

Then suddenly, Dad died also! The last time I saw him, he went striding past our front window on a Saturday morning as if there was some urgent business that needed to be seen to. But that was just standard procedure for him, as he didn't know how to walk slowly, even in his eighty-seventh year! He'd been a true *grafter* all of his life! What and where he was heading for I still don't know, but he succumbed that evening having suffered a heart attack and didn't make it to the hospital. RIP.

Life goes on . . . again.

Archie's golf ball mould was kept busy in the evenings, and we were successfully churning out good quality gutta balls. There was plenty of potential here for a cottage industry in its own right by selling the really good mouldings, and it was a win-win situation because the not so good ones could be used on the course, for play. So long as we could source good quality gutta, there was a buck to be made here, even though the gutta wasn't cheap!

Another fantastic boost for the actual experience was when Barry sent down a few free samples of a ball which was available from the old Penfold Company in Birmingham. Penfold were one of the leading ball manufacturers for decades, and I can remember playing with them myself in my heyday (what heyday?).

They were actually a very good ball to play with, but they were unforgettably as soft as shit! One mishit and the balata ball was virtually deemed useless with a gaping smile on its face. Thankfully, these balls were made to replicate the mesh pattern balls of the 1920s-1930s era and were highly durable. Now we had two types of early golf balls which were indisputably ideal for the job! One difficult and one easy—both perfect, almost!

Barry had also sent a set of the proposed Nicoll clubs we were interested in buying. A fun day was promised on the first good day given to us in January 1999. And that good day arrived on a Saturday morning, and Harry and myself got armed with our hickories, a few of our own guttas and the lattice pattern Penfolds which would simulate a typical ball of the 1920s. My, my! The entire package comprising clubs, balls, and the course was certainly coming together in theory.

Now it was time to see if the golf package worked in practice. In effect, the two wee boys had been reincarnated again, as we strutted up towards the first tee. In reality, ageing bones were creaking and perplexed muscles were prepared for an activity that hadn't arisen for quite a while—swinging a golf club!

Practice swings were taken, and impressive swishes could be heard in the village a mile away, I'm sure. This was only a fact-finding exercise to gauge the distance two moderate hitters could propel the two types of ball we had. The greens were nowhere near at a puttable condition, which certainly suited me and saved the usual embarrassment of three putting.

We had played a few shots in the past with our modern garbage, but now it was show time, for real. And you know what—it was just another game of golf, except in a different era. Yes, we shared a few duffs and foozles here and there, but generally we both did rather well. Anyway, it wasn't out of the ordinary for us to have a wee foozle wi' Big Bertha what's-her-name! If *we* were having fun, then so could anyone!

Our guttas were performing just as they probably should. We were lucky if we got 170 yards out of a good drive, and the buggers were difficult to get airborne, while they felt like you were taking a whack at a pebble. The lattice patterns on the other hand were probably just as they should be too! They were much easier and softer to strike with the benefit of the extra twenty yards or so.

The lattice balls were made from some sort of compound, although they were not the same as the old putty balls you used to get. Both of us retired full in the satisfaction that we now had an experience worth selling! With the fun over, it was a case of getting back to the tidying up process and the making of bridges for crossing points.

The following day, Ross had recruited the help of some of his pals, wee Chris Porter, Grant and David McMorran, and Kevin Robison, and we set about clearing stones from the broken turf at the ditches. There was to be some great excitement not long after we had started because I found a gutta ball at the area close to the middle pond! It was a 'Silvertown' mesh pattern gutty from the 1890s and in fairly good condition, but with hardly a speck of paint left on its surface.

This was a common failing of the gutta-percha balls throughout their entire history; they just didn't like a good lick of paint. After a wee lecture at Ross and the boys about the find, I boasted, 'See! You've got to keep your eyes open and maybe you'll find one too! Right! Get back tae work ya wee buggers!'

By March 1999, Graham had put out a 600-strong mail run to golf clubs and selected businesses in the hope of sparking some interest and our first customers for the summer months. Prospective sponsors that Harry and Graham had been chasing up just didn't want to get involved. This was really disappointing considering golf in general is heavily supported at both professional and amateur levels. I continued my own programme of helping Jim at the caravan park to earn a few bob and then going up to the course till dark. Graham was beginning to look a bit conspicuous by his absence.

Here we were at the threshold of another summer, and we still weren't ready in all departments. We'd be chancing our luck by accepting customers at this time. I was losing all patience with my partners and was totally pissed off!

Then just when I was beginning to think that all was lost, we had a meeting at the course to try and iron out the obvious shortcomings hanging over our heads, and the course, like a dark cloud! Surprise, surprise. Everybody was still on board, but we had to get ourselves bloody motivated—or put the whole thing off for another year.

Harry had managed to get a small web site up and running through a computer guy he was friendly with, and Graham was making enquiries with a local development company for possible funding. Harry had also secured a major freebie through *Bunkered Magazine*, who were impressed by our work to date and who were going to do a four-page feature in their next issue. The article would cover the local golf history and the Arbory Brae hickory golf venture.

Their correspondent, Scott Crockett, was penned in for a visit to the course in the near future to interview Harry and myself, and Graham if he wanted to be there. And that third green was still bereft of topsoil and turf!

So another survey of the course was carried out by Harry and myself, resulting in a 'must do' list of vital works needing action as soon as possible. The nights were drawing out again, and we would be able to get a few hours in each night. This list we had before us would have scared the life out of most people, but it was all doable so long as we kept picking away at it.

Looking back now, our sweat equity at this point was not merely hundreds of hours on and off the course—it was thousands! We were up to our necks in a labour of love, but it certainly wasn't a love of labour.

A wee stroke of luck came our way when Tam Lammie and Sandy Reive from the village informed us that a demolishing firm was knocking down the old schoolhouse at Leadhills and they were looking for somewhere to dump the rubble. Yes! We would have that, free of charge of course, and they could dump it at our proposed parking area on the Coldchapel road. Then we would just have stick in and shift the estimated 100 tons to all the areas on the course still requiring access crossing points. And that meant getting access to that third bloody green, at last! Access! Access! Access!

Scott Crockett came and interviewed us at the course for something like three to four hours and left sincerely impressed with the whole set-up. He also had other media contacts which he passed on to us, which would prove fruitful in the future—Harry's department. There's no doubt about it. Harry was in his element when it came down to all this marketing and promotional stuff.

I kept plodding away on the course with help from Harry, Ross, and his pals, and by now, I had found five old balls, the quality of which was depreciating fast. A couple were wound balls, and their balata covers had perished so much that the resulting finds were spewing out their elasticated guts! It still gave an adrenalin rush when you found one though. I always hoped that Harry would eventually uncover one for himself—and then he would forgive me for the Carluke affair.

The rubble started coming in from Leadhills, and being a builder, I immediately spotted an opportunity for a possible building project of the future. As this considerable heap would have to be hand-balled into Jim's wee dumper truck, I graded all the best building stone and kept it to the side. No sense in wasting good stone. *Use what you've got, and you'll never be without!*

What a boost this was to the inner egos of all concerned! We were starting to make our way over that bloody ditch to the third green. A concerted effort over four evenings' work saw us over the ditch, and such was the ecstasy of Harry and Ross that they drove the wee dumper in laps of honour all around that which had been until now virgin ground that had never seen our dumper truck! The eagle had landed, and the next target was to get the topsoil up and levelled off and then turf the green.

The course and its greens were now at a stage where we needed some professional consultation on the subject of nurturing and looking after them, especially the greens. Neither Harry nor myself was an expert green-keeper, but as it happened, my next-door neighbour, George Hendry, was an expert green-keeper and worked at Biggar golf course at the time.

George had already been helping us with a few odds and ends and had been keeping us right—from a distance. It was now time for George to make a site visit and give his opinions. He did come up on a Sunday at the end of March, when we had the notepad at the ready, and he went through the A-Z of green keeping in a crash course over a few hours!

George was another grafter, and I remember Harry and I playing golf at Biggar on a raw early winter day and coming across him. He was top dressing a green and the sweat was pissing off his brow, and he only had a T-shirt on his back!

George advised us to start feather raking the greens in order to free the moss which was starting to get into our good grass. It was not totally surprising as the whole golf course was one big beautiful expanse of soft springy turf, thanks to the moss content within it! We truly hated this task, as it drew the guts out of you, pulling and scratching with that damn rake.

Again, there was the easy option of hiring a petrol scarifier which would get the job done far quickly, more thoroughly, but more expensively. Shit happens! We were both getting rather sick and tired of all the work having to be done—the hard way. And time was marching on, as it does.

We had a meeting with Graham at the course, and he explained his absence was because of his own work commitments, and even worse, he couldn't see the situation getting any better. He would let us know in the near future as to whether he could stay with the project or reluctantly drop out.

Both Harry and I had mixed feelings about Graham's input, but we simply couldn't afford any passengers, and I know Graham understood that too. Whether Graham had thought that the venture had no future at this stage, I don't know. He had, nonetheless, put considerable time and money into Arbory and his efforts were greatly appreciated.

As far as Duncan was concerned, he was still with us and was patient with regard to some payment for the lease and helped where he could with plant and machinery shifting road scalpings (his road scalpings) to blind off the crossing points. He even brought us a ten-gallon drum of diesel for the dumper truck. The whole family were so supportive, but as Duncan used to say now and again as a reminder to Harry and me, 'in the end, everything has tae pay for itself!'

The *Bunkered Magazine* article was out in the paper racks and hopefully selling well. Oh, for some feedback and some customers maybe. We kept plodding on, making progress, and Harry even found his first gutta! Sad to say, it was one which we ourselves lost when we had been having our fun hickory golf day a month back. Never mind, it's a start. Better luck next time, H.

On the same theme, I found another gutty on May Day 1999, and this time it was a cracker in almost pristine condition! Both Harry and I had been working in the same area about ten yards apart, and there it was just waiting for me to find it.

All these finds were coming from the scrapings when the ditches were cleaned by Sam. We'd had the usual deluge of rainstorms, and this is what actually exposed this ball. If he'd been that wee bit more alert this find, a Silvertown mesh with a good covering of paint intact could have been his. Ah well, to the victor the spoils, eh!

I must have been taking the piss and bragging over this latest find because I was heading for a reality check the next day. Ross was helping as usual because it was a Sunday, and the bugger caught me hook, line, and sinker. Remember that dirty trick I played on Harry at Carluke? Well, this was payback time, and the two of them had been in collusion with each other to bring the big yin back down to earth.

We were all working tirelessly in a ditch at the third hole and I was in the ditch with my wellies on when I spied the latest little treasure sitting ever so cosy on the banking. 'Now this is exactly what I've been telling the two of you about!' I shouted.

They both turned and stared at me. 'What are you going on about?' Ross asked quite innocently.

'Look! Look there! Now the two of you went up here just a minute ago and both of you must be bloody blind!' I declared with my usual arrogance at making a find. I had deliberately left the . . . object on the banking to stress my point of being observant to the find. I pointed at the ball and bent over to pick it up gently with thumb and forefinger.

'Ah don't know. I must just have a natural talent for finding . . . ya bastards!' My fingers were sinking into this ball as they might do with some soft chocolate! I thought the two of them were going to rupture themselves from the exertion of their laughter directed straight at me. The ball was one made of pure muck which Ross had craftily rolled and modelled into an impressive replica of the real thing. Buggers! I didn't hear the end of their coup de grâce for some time after that.

The three of us continued to put in long hours on the course, as and when each was available. Weekends were normally two full shifts, morning till night, but the rewards could be seen before our eyes after each and every shift. Harry's contacts with the newspapers started to yield a list of free articles and features with one leading on to another, and another, and another, and then the radio, and then TV!

It was a wee bit like the rise of Citizen Kane, but not quite so prolific. The photographic shoots I could handle easily. TV and radio were a lot more nerve-racking for someone who was content to hide in the background. Harry took these things in his stride and got a buzz from the experience. For me, there was no place to hide, and I accepted that it had to be done!

Of course, all this free publicity was marvellous, but they were essentially one hit wonders. The TV spot was a Scottish television newsreel supplement that went out soon after it was shot in the morning. It made the lunchtime, teatime, and late evening newscasts. The reporter was Christina MacIntyre, who was obviously a good golfer and managed to hole a stymie shot—but unfortunately not on camera. Mum's flags were seen wavering in the soft breeze that day which was thought-provoking for Harry, Ross, and myself.

The summer heat was drying out the greens, and they were noticeably, badly in need of water, especially the third green because of the time we took in getting it laid with turf. It still looked very tired looking but recovering well. What we needed here was a piece of improvisation.

We had noticed spring water coming from the hillside about forty yards above the green. Gravity was on our side, and so we dug a small reservoir to trap the trickle of spring water and stuck a hosepipe into the pool and let gravity do the rest. Once the water siphoned through the hosepipe, there was just enough pressure to turn a garden sprinkler head and spread a spray of water across the green. We were seldom stuck for a solution, and as far as fresh water was concerned, we had loads in those two ponds that Harry had pushed for.

Graham had requested a meeting at the course, and we duly obliged. Just as we had thought, he was there to tell us that he was throwing in the towel due to his growing work commitments and how there was no way in which he could give the project the time needed. I have to confess about feeling rather guilty about Graham's departure from the business. Perhaps I was responsible for putting pressure on him because of his lack of presence at the course. I felt that Graham was now holding us back, after helping us greatly to get to where we were now.

The valuable work he put in could not be underestimated, and that included work on the course too! But he had bigger fish to fry with his golf architecture commitments and his partnership in Kames golf course. He was a Sassenach, just like my late father was, and as a businessman, he was very much in the 'we have to be careful' mould.

I just believed that—after having gone so far down this road we were travelling—time was of the essence for getting this business up and running. For Harry and me, it was a lifeline and opportunity for a new shot at a working life, you know—*find a job you like doing, and you'll never work another day in your life!* For Graham, it was more like a spare time hobby.

Nearing the end of June, we had Peter Strachan from Radio Scotland doing a recorded interview on the course. I was OK with this because it wasn't going out live, unlike Wayne Riley who at the 1991 PGA Championship was asked on live radio, 'So what do you do in your spare time, Wayne?'

Quick as a flash, he said, 'Sex! . . . This isn't live, is it?'

Peter arrived one night, and we played round the course with him recording as we advanced hole by hole. I think Peter, who looked like a bit of a golfer, was having trouble coming to grips with what he was seeing. The interview went well with various jocular remarks being made throughout. Peter mentioned the presence of the sheep meandering all over the course and asked if they would be a permanent fixture.

'Oh aye,' said Harry 'They're our main grass cutters and have a function to do!'

To which, Peter replied rather astutely, 'Aye. It looks like there are functions all over the place!' He was referring to the sheep shit. This was becoming more and more fun all the time, and I was just about starting to enjoy these brief encounters with mini stardom.

The next encounter came only a week later when my wife's cousin, Ian Turner, arrived at the course to do another interview for Radio Scotland. This time, however, the gig was live at ten in the morning. A phone connection was required in order to relay the event back to the studio for some live interaction with the studio host.

Ian arrived early to set up the phone connection after which we engaged in some banter. We gave Ian some insight as to what this experience was all about and how it came about. Then, just before going on live, we told him about our exploits in my wife's kitchen making those gutta balls and the stench of boiling gutta, etc.

'But don't bring that up, Ian, or I'll have my head to play with!' I hastily pleaded before it was star party time again.

Well, the whole hour was full of fun, when nearing the end Ian asked me, 'And what's all this about abusing your wife's kitchen by making smelly gutta golf balls in your house, Alfie?'

That took me aback and I was stuttering, 'Eh. Aye, well, eh . . . I told you not to bring that up, Ian!' I said, while we all broke into laughter which was echoed by the studio laughter we could hear through our earpieces. What fun!

Surely all this media attention had to pay off. The good thing was that there was no sign of this attention calming down as article after article was written about us somewhere on the planet! And there was even better to come later on.

We needed thousands of promotional leaflets, and Harry came good by gaining a handsome £750 sponsor for these. The legendary John Panton made a visit to the course and was full of compliments for what we were trying to do. And we held an open day attended by our friend, Sandy Sinclair, past captain of the R&A, but poorly attended by anyone else—about twelve others in all!

We'd hired a small marquis to host the anticipated visitors, and I think this highlighted one last major weakness in the whole set-up—that we didn't have a decent facility for our guests. With no bookings coming in from a range of our efforts; including mail runs and all this media attention, we were becoming baffled, and concerned, as to why those badly needed customers were failing to appear. Build it and the people will come! Really?

Going into November 1999, we began searching for some kind of second-hand shed that would suffice in the meantime as a small clubhouse. By the end of the month, Harry had found a real possibility at Roslin, home of the famous Roslin Chapel near Edinburgh, which was indeed quite a large shed, presently used as a children's nursery.

Having gone through to inspect the building, the only problem lay in the cost that the vendors were looking for—£3,600! The timber frame structure had a pitched roof and was of an 'L' shaped design with forty-five square metres of floor space to play with, and it could be easily adapted to suit, and most critically, our customers' needs. I am a builder, after all—and with Harry being an electrician come labourer for all things, this was all very doable! What's more, the actual design of this cabin-like structure was in every way typical of an early clubhouse facility.

A meeting was required. We spoke with Duncan, our last remaining partner, and he agreed that we should offer £2800 and take it at £3000.

Deal done, Duncan would arrange to have it brought back to Abington on his lorry after we'd gone through to dismantle it. Having taken all the dimensions of the cabin, I got started with the drawing of plans which would have to be submitted to our pals at the planning department, again.

Time was of the essence, and I had hoped, rather optimistically, that we might just get our consent rushed through in the name of Scottish tourism. No chance! They dug in, and we had to wait months before we could start erecting our new pavilion which had to sit in pieces, covered in polythene, in our car park area.

As things were getting somewhat drastic in the financial stakes, I had begun a campaign of communicating with our great Scottish political leaders who were, unfortunately for us, kiddie-on socialists. Henry McLeish was First Minister at this time, who demanded 'service, service, service' from the tourist industry. Who better to write to than someone in power whose heart was in the future of our tourism industry?

We did get a response eventually from a manservant, which amounted to nothing more than a diplomatic back-heel job on to our Tourism Board, which didn't have a single penny in their budget to accommodate any form of funding. Thanks for nothing, Henry! I suppose we should have been thankful for any kind of response from our highest political dignitary. Oh, the rascal!

Then in December, Duncan, our last surviving partner at World Heritage Links Ltd, decided to withdraw from any further interest in the running of the business and resigned from his directorship. He continued to wish us luck with the venture but stated that he and the family had 'bigger fish to fry in their farming businesses'.

And then there were two! Harry and I had become the sole owners of the company, which didn't leave me feeling all too reassured. Nobody could dispute our work rate, but our acumen in business matters lacked a certain ruthless streak which would have paid dividends. We would simply have to plod on the best we could.

The planners continued to hold us back in their usual bureaucratic fashion, and we had begun a serious clean-up of the sheep shit that had multiplied and gathered over the past months. When March appeared, we weighed up the planning situation and decided to build the foundations in advance. To hell wi' them!

There was nothing we could say that would help the situation along, even though they full well knew the urgency required on our part. I've been dealing with these rascals for more than twenty years in the building trade, and still they wallow in their own self-importance? Oh, some more rascals! Harry and I plodded on in horrible weather, building those simple foundations, and we filmed some videos as a record. Harry asked, 'Do you think we should send this to McLeish?'

'Aye!' I said angrily. 'Are ye watching, Henry? This is how you do your bit for Scottish tourism!' And I literally threw my trowel and its mortar contents at the wall we were busy building. Ping and splat! A little moment of tantrum, but one which alleviated the pressure on both of us for a short while as we laughed away grudgingly.

Eventually, consent was approved, and we got stuck into erecting our pavilion. Scott Jamieson, of the spiteful rabbit comment, came up and gave us a welcome hand to lay the floor and get the sides up. We would need Duncan to assist in lifting the roof sections on to the walls and then we could get it 'wind and watertight'.

There were four sections to the roof, and the first three went up easily. The last piece, for the 'L' part, proved more difficult as Duncan couldn't reach completely over the parts already built. All he could do was to perch this final piece precariously on top of the built section, because that was as far as the forklift could reach. Harry and I would have to manhandle the last heavy piece into place ourselves.

With grunts and groans, we nudged this final section down on to the wall head in preparation for the next manoeuvre and then went inside to assess the next move. Hopefully, we could safely slide it along the wall head and into place. The process facing us was fairly simple, but not entirely safe! We were directly underneath this heavy lump of timber, and if either edge were to slip off the wall head as we were nudging it along, then someone would get squashed!

We had the camcorder filming our precarious activities, and for whatever reason, I decided to go and switch it off. As I approached the camera, I peered into the lens and said, 'This next bit is a wee bit too dangerous for you people at home!' and switched it off. Maybe I was just being careful by not filming the demise of two crazy brothers.

Once the preliminary strategy was agreed upon, we synchronised spurts of energy and successfully got the damn thing into place ready for nailing and making sound. To say we were relieved to get this task out of the way would be an understatement. But we got the job done and without any personal injury! We then took some more footage for posterity—and had a well-earned fag.

One of the stipulations from the Building Control was that we carried out a porosity test of the ground in order to satisfy the laying of a proposed soakaway drain. A load of bullshit in some ways, but necessary in the name of building regulations. This involved digging a hole in the ground and filling it up with water and then recording the time it took for the water to soak away naturally into the ground. I think I had to do this three times, and after the second time, I left my empty bucket at the hole in readiness for repeating the exercise the next day.

The next morning, I went to retrieve the bucket to fill it up with water for the last test. As I bent down to pick it up—croak! What the hell—croak, croak! There were two bloody enormous puddocks (frogs) in the bottom of the bucket. Not only that—they were going at it, good style! Bugger this, I thought, and perhaps out of pure jealousy, I tipped the buggers on to the ground where they were reluctant to disassociate themselves. So when I returned with the water, they got a good splash of icy cold water that seemed to do the trick! Damned cheeky puddocks!

The next major step in getting the pavilion complete entailed getting the drains dug and installed; securing and sealing the roof; erecting partitions to convert the interior to give a small toilet, small kitchen, and ample lounge area; and then to line the entire interior with a mixture of plasterboard walls and pine-clad ceilings.

This building, when complete, would not be getting dismantled again—it was here to stay! Our wee pavilion would serve as the last piece in the puzzle, at least, for the time being.

In the beginning of April, we had a visit from Keith Grieve, a producer with BBC Scotland, who was making a new programme called *Outside Now*. Keith came to see us and evaluate the possibilities of filming at Arbory for inclusion in the programme. Having spent a couple of hours interviewing us and trying to understand the unique experience we were trying to sell, he conveyed some heartening comments for a non-golfer.

Harry got in first as he asked him, 'Well, Keith, what do you think of this place and what are the chances of filming here?'

Without any hesitation, he replied, 'Oh, I think the place is brilliant, and I'll definitely be recommending that we come back here to film. You know, I had thought we could get four minutes air time out of this. The reality is, I could do a full one-hour programme on your golf course!'

'What! Really?' Harry said excitedly.

'Absolutely, Harry. But there's no way I would be allowed to do that, although I'm sure we'll be upping the stakes from the original four-minute plan!'

It was now a case of wait and see, although it did look like a certainty that they would be back in May with Hazel Irvine, the show's presenter. Keith had hinted that they would require a full day's shoot at Arbory and asked us if we could arrange a period costume for Hazel. Our local theatre workshop at Biggar gave us a variety of wear from which Hazel could choose for herself.

The interior of the pavilion was nearing completion and more than looked the part with an array of historical golf images decorating the walls. Harry had finished wiring the place out, and although we couldn't afford the astronomical fees for a direct mains electricity supply, Ronnie had given us a loan of his generator which not only booted up all the lights but was also good enough to boil the kettle in quick time!

Ronnie would also be coming up sometime to erect a wooden bench seat along the lounge wall and assist with other joinery projects. In return for his help, I had promised to build the foundations of a conservatory he was erecting. As to how I would find the time I would worry about later.

Everything was progressing well, but the pressure of having insufficient funds was hurting both of us and the business. We were also on our own now, which was disconcerting because neither of us was a budding entrepreneur or salesman!

I need a wee break from the keyboard—and the obligatory fag, of course! The cigar smoking and amiable Miguel Jimenez of Spain had a nice little quote: '*Caffeine plus nicotine equals protein!*' But these days that has to be exercised outside in the open air. Dirty smokers an' all that, and quite right too, I must reluctantly concede, although it's not too distressing on a mild clear night when stargazing blends so pleasantly with the puffing routine.

Isn't all that vastness of infinite space so mind-boggling? I always seem to reflect upon how miniscule and insignificant we all are—and yet how important we think we are. Aye, the smokin' ban has helped me to cut down a bit and scan the depths of our universe much more than I would have.

Orion, Pegasus, the Plough pointing to Polaris, Perseus with its annual meteor showers (usually on thick cloudy nights), Gemini—and on a rare occasion, I see a slow moving star ambling its way over the night sky . . . or would that be the space station? And what lies behind Orion's belt or any of the above? Only another million tiny specs of light! Maybe golf isn't all that important.

> But brightly beams aboon them a'
> The star o' Rabbie Burns.

Oh, the better wonders of evolving mankind and the simple wonderment of wondering and wonder! Christ! I'd hate to be blind and miss out on the clear night spectacle, even though it's been a while since the 20-20 vision helped me at snooker. Aye—age disnae come itsel'!

Golf's Dilemma—the Ball!

Before we continue further, I feel it's essential to give a brief account of one of golf's greatest assets–the ball, and most important of all, the effects of the ball in relation to the sport through the various stages of golf's evolution. Fundamentally, as the ball evolved, then so did the sport in general! The ball was the leader and the implements, or clubs, followed every time the ball was improved.

The earliest factual accounts relating to the ball was Thomas Mathieson's poem–'The Goff'–dating back to 1743. Mathieson describes the making of a feathery golf ball in considerable detail, a ball which was made (usually) with a casing of leather, bull, or horse hide and then stuffed full with goose or chicken feathers. The standard quantity of feathers required for each ball has been stated as '*a top hat filled full of feathers to the brim of the hat*', but whether there is any accuracy to this measure is neither here nor there.

Prior to the feather ball, we have to enter into the realms of subjectivity where it is commonly believed that wood was used or, as our old pal Archie Baird would claim, golfers used the cork floats from old fishing nets. A sound suggestion considering early golf existed primarily on the seaside links of the east coast of Scotland.

The making of the feather balls was a slow and laborious work of art with a good ball maker only turning out three or four balls in a day. Many ball makers would suffer from serious chest problems later in life due to the damage caused by the pressing tool they used to force the feathers home. Harry and I had often dreamt of having a go with a feathery, but we both knew the likelihood of that ever happening wasn't all that realistic.

That was until Neil Hunter, our faithful and dedicated member, appeared at the course one night, and we played a few holes before retiring to the pavilion for a cuppa. I made up a brew, and we sat down for a good natter as was, by now, standard procedure. Neil looked at both of us rather sheepishly and said, 'I've got something to show you. But I don't want you to laugh when you see it.'

We were baffled by Neil's statement, and I replied, 'Och, no. We wouldna dae that, Neil. What is it you want us to see?'

He reached nervously into his pocket. 'Well, do you remember we were talking about the feather balls a few weeks back?'

'Aye. Ah remember,' Harry said and I nodded in agreement.

'Well, I thought I would try and make one, but it didn't quite work out as planned,' he said with a hint of humility while producing this *thing* from his pocket. It was the shape and size of a 'double yoker' hen's egg, and it looked as though the poor hen's arse was still sticking to it!

'That's . . . ehm . . . well, it's . . . eh . . . fuckin' scary, Neil!' And we all laughed heartily.

Once we'd calmed down Neil looked at me as though he needed some words of comfort.

'Actually, Neil, I think what you've produced here is absolutely bloody marvellous!'

'How's that?' he asked. 'You're going to take the piss, aren't you?'

'No. Not at all, Neil,' I replied while fondling this weird, but dead creature in my hands. 'This is exactly what we need to demonstrate to our customers how a feathery would look when the stitching had burst open and started to yield its feathery interior. Well done! Can I keep this . . . thing?'

'Of course you can. It was meant for you anyway,' he said as we all continued to have a good laugh.

And so it was, whereby that *thing* provoked many a raised eyebrow from the customers. Neil had actually done rather well in this . . . his first attempt, his prototype, at being a feather ball maker. I knew full well that he would persevere and come strutting back some day with a round and completely stitched-up feather ball. I couldn't wait, because his next effort would be getting a fair old wallop with the brassie! The prototype looked as though it might not hold together if it was accidentally dropped on the floor.

The feather balls were highly volatile and very expensive, costing more than the price of a golf club! Hence, the sport was far too expensive for most to take part in, especially as the short lifespan of each ball meant that a player would sometimes require at least six per round! And because the balls were so volatile, it meant that only wooden-headed clubs, or playclubs as they were called, could be used, including one for the art of putting. One metal-headed club was used called a 'rut' iron, but this was only for extreme situations where the ball had to be extricated from very bad lies such as cart tracks. *Play the ball as it lies and take the course as you find it!*

On the plus side, hitting a feathery was a pure joy. But if this sport of golf was ever going to expand its pleasures to more people, then the game needed something revolutionary to happen, and that *would* happen with the advent of balls made from gutta-percha.

A good deal of our time went into this area of research, because the gutta-percha balls were key to giving the customer a genuinely authentic nineteenth-century golf experience at Arbory. If we could, somehow, reproduce our own guttas, then that would be a massive breakthrough for the project!

We already knew that David Hamilton of St Andrews was busy researching and making his brand of gutta balls, and therefore he became the first port of call for assistance. I think it was Archie who tipped us off about David's exploits with gutta because we had secured the use of Archie's Willie Park golf ball mould to make our own gutta balls.

Anyway, we got in touch with David, and he duly sent us various bits of information, including a text draft of his new book—*Precious Gum*—which gave a complete history of the gutta-percha era relating to the ball. This I considered a marvellous and highly trusting gesture, but at the same time, I felt a wee bit miffed that David had beaten me to the punch on this one. I had thought about trying to write up the history of gutta-percha myself at some later date.

The name gutta-percha actually means 'tree sap' in Malayan. It's the sap or resin which was extracted from various species of the gutta-percha tree (Palaquium) in the early nineteenth century. Once its unique properties were discovered, it soon became a highly sought after commercial product and was used extensively to insulate the first undersea telegraphic cables which would encircle the world.

Unfortunately, the early means of extraction saw the gutta-percha forests being decimated, courtesy of the massive demand for the gum. The method of extraction was crude and unnecessary because the local natives would chop the trees down and then extract the valuable gum from the trunk, amounting to only fourteen kilograms per tree in some instances.

Sadly, they discovered too late that the gum could be extracted in a similar manner as rubber by making incisions in the bark and collecting the juice in small trays or alternately by processing the juice from the leaves by simply plucking them from the trees.

Once the new technologies for insulating the undersea cables were discovered for which India rubber was more extensively used, golf ball manufacture became the main product for gutta-percha use. It was estimated in 1892 that 500 tons of gutta was used annually for this purpose, which equated to nearly 12,000,000 balls annually! Although perhaps overstated, the amount was still considerable and underlined the growth of golf as a sport.

The Reverend Dr R. Paterson of St Andrews is generally given credit for inventing the gutta ball, although this is disputed by historians. Regardless, it *was* invented, and possibly as early as 1845. By 1848, the celebrated song 'In Praise of Gutta Percha' had been written by W. Graham of Edinburgh, which recorded the arrival of gutta balls and their welcome impact on the sport. He described the feather balls and the advent of gutta thus:

And though our best wi' them we tried,
And nicely every club applied,
They whirred and fuffed, and dooked and shied,
And sklentit into bunkers.

But times are changed—we dinna care
Though we may ne'er drive leather mair,
Be't stuffed wi' feathers or wi' hair—
For noo we're independent.
At last a substance we hae got
Frae which, for scarce mair than a groat,
A ba' comes that can row and sto—
A ba' the most transcendent.
Hail! GUTTA PERCHA, *precious gum!*

Gutta as a material becomes malleable when softened in hot water and returns to its original hard state when allowed to cool due to its extraordinary property of molecular memory. The first gutta balls were simply hand-rolled, giving a smooth finish, and although a boon to the sport and its players, their flight was highly irregular.

The first improvement to the new gutta ball came totally by accident. The players soon realised that the more a ball got hacked and scraped with play the better it performed. This discovery led to deliberate scoring and hand-hammering of the balls to give them markings. Eventually, the moulding process was introduced, giving a regular and uniform product.

As there was no rule governing the size of a ball throughout the gutta era, old scuffed-up balls could be remoulded using a slightly smaller mould. It wasn't until the R&A became official custodians of the rules in 1897 that the size of a golf ball was set at no less than 1.62 inches in diameter and no more than 1.62 ounces in weight.

Considering golf's affinity with nature, it might be thought that these sizes were completely appropriate and correct when related to Fibonacci's golden numbers of natural law. Now there's something to think about.

Forever Chasing Rainbows and Funding

The May Day holiday had arrived, and Harry was trying to muster up a group of journalists to come and play at the course with a view to getting even more press coverage. In hindsight, it turned out to be a bad idea to hold this sort of thing on a bank holiday. That said, the lads from *Bunkered Magazine* turned up along with a couple of tour operators, who had shown interest in the attraction.

Harry was notably disappointed by the attendance, but he shouldn't have been. One of Scotland's most respected golf writers, Mike Aitken of *The Scotsman*, appeared and played seven holes before stating that he just had to get back home to Edinburgh to his family, who were waiting for him to spend some quality time on the holiday. Being a capable golfer, he had enjoyed his game and confessed that he hadn't been sure what to expect on the visit.

However, he departed delighted with the experience and gave us a good write-up soon after. The day was far from being a disaster, but we still needed those customers as the funds had been exhausted again! People began to filter up to the course for a look-see, and general enquiry rates increased, but we had to find some way of getting golfers who were prepared to part with their hard-earned cash! Crazy as it may seem, I went off to start building Ronnie's founds after everybody had left and worked till dark. Yes—this was indeed crazy, especially as the BBC was heading our way the next day to bestow upon us another minute of fame.

Thankfully, the Big Man blessed wee Arbory with a beautiful early summer day and bathed the course in warm sunshine. Mum had made us nine white flags before she went into hospital, and they were holding up well in condition. They made me think how they seemed to sum up the whole affair with Arbory—an elaborate patchwork quilt built on the cheap, cutting corners at every turn in order to save a penny here and there. And yet we had reached our final goal by restoring an insignificant piece of farmland back to its former glory, of wanting to be a golf course.

What could we have done with some real cash and proper funding? Those flags wavered in the breeze and gave us both a sense of triumphalism and pride! They looked just like Robin Williams had hilariously described them—all fluttering away on wee bits of *flat ground, just to give the golfer* (Harry and me), *a little bit of fuckin' hope.'*

Hazel, Keith, and the rest of the team arrived about nine in the morning, and Hazel got herself kitted out in a costume. My nerves had been jangling since I had woken that morning, and Harry was feeling a bit edgy too! Matters weren't helped by the fact that both of us were completely rundown and worn out by the whole effort of setting up this business. But we were both adamant that this was going to be a real fun day!

Keith gave us a preliminary briefing on some of the angles he wanted to try and capture, and after appropriate make-up was applied, we all went out on to the course. To be an international star came fairly natural to Harry. As far as I was concerned, well, they had to use more film because of the extra takes required from my fluffs. Hazel was brilliant, and what a learning curve it was to see her at work. Keith would narrate the intended sketch for five minutes, then ask her if she was OK with that. Then she just rattled the lot off her cuff like she'd known the different details and facts all her life. Very impressive stuff! Maybe it helped that she was a very able golfer.

They were filming here, there, and everywhere with Harry and I being invited before the camera every now and again to make our thespian contributions, with aspirations of an Oscar just round the corner. Things were being filmed about which we hadn't the foggiest clue as to what they were about. We found out later that they were actually doing the trailers for the programme's launch!

Such exposure we couldn't have dreamt of paying for, and everything was proving a real bonus to what we were expecting. I've never ceased from being embarrassed at the thought of how I asked them for payment for our services! Well, we were desperate and every pound was a prisoner for the venture.

An interesting topic arose when we were having lunch in the pavilion. Harry and I had been explaining to Keith the special properties of the gutta balls and how they floated in water. For some reason, which became apparent later in the afternoon, Keith latched on to this aspect of ye olde gem. 'And what did you do if your ball landed in water all those years back?' he asked.

'Well,' Harry said, 'they had a saying in those days, "*Play the ball as lies, and take the course as you find it!*" They just had to play the ball off the top of the water, and they had special implements for that very purpose, called unsurprisingly water irons.'

Nothing more was said of it, until late in the afternoon when they were obviously nearing completion of the shoot. Keith beckoned us over for a word and asked, 'Remember we were talking about the gutta balls and how they floated on water?'

'Aye?'

'Do you have one with you?'

'Aye.'

Then he shared his devious plot to get one over on Hazel, on film of course, whereby he was going to ask her to play a water shot, the idea being that poor wee Hazel would end up being well drenched through by her efforts to extricate the ball from Harry's pond!

'Aye! Not a bad idea, Keith,' exclaimed Harry as we all laughed.

Hazel was then summoned towards the pond where all (well, nearly all) was explained for the last shot of the day. She was readily up for the task and got herself into position, taking her stance at the very edge of the water. Harry and I had been given our lines, and we placed the gutta in the water and watched it bob up and down in the slight disturbance on the surface. Action!

'So what do I do with this, guys?' she asked.

'Well,' said Harry, 'I think you'll just have to play it as it lies.'

'OK, then,' she replied as she started her backswing, and Harry and I backed away in the background, in anticipation of a watery outcome.

Swish, then splash! Nobody could believe the result. She had managed to sweep the ball clean off the top of the water and thirty yards over the small pond. And not a bloody speck of water could be seen on her entire body! Well done, Hazel, but I think she actually wasted the real plot.

That was it, and Keith went walkabout on his own, to take a few film shots from all over the course. Hazel, Harry, and I sat down on a sleeper bridge with our legs dangling over the side, with Harry and I puffing away and telling her the real story of Arbory and our struggle to survive. The pressure, if there really was any, was off and we could all relax now.

What a fun day it was, with Hazel stating how she herself had loved the day out at Arbory. On this occasion, the weather had been kind to us, and what a difference that made.

Periodically, over the next couple of weeks, we would see the *Outside Now* trailer on the Beeb until the programme was finally aired. It looked all right from our perspective, and Keith's four-minute spot finished up at around fourteen minutes of airtime in a thirty-minute programme! I reckoned that kinda spoke for itself!

The Beeb had done us a great favour, and our pay cheques came in the post—fifty quid each, which I wish to hell I had never asked for in the first place. Desperate times and desperate measures by a couple of desperados!

Our brief encounter with fun was over again, and it was back to business as usual. Shit pickin' on a grand scale was required before we found ourselves overwhelmed with . . . shit! The company funds were at an all-time low again. In fact, we were totally skint. Nevertheless, we went to Lanark to look at a small tractor which we thought could be converted in some way which would pick up the sheep shit without breaking our backs and consuming all of our time. It didn't work out, so it was back to the gloves and buckets.

Then one morning when we had arranged a breath-wasting meeting at Lanark with the Clydesdale Development Association for a funding lifeline, I nearly met my maker. I had slept in and was running late for making to another meeting of futile nothingness. I knew before I got there what the first and premier request would be—cash-flow projections!

Being late and having only ten minutes to navigate the twelve miles, I did what most would do in the same situation. I put the foot hard on the metal. I knew the road like the back of my hand and also my limitations as a driver at speed. Coming along a straight with a gentle bend at the end of it, I was in total control until I saw a farm tractor and trailer starting to inch its way across the road about 600 yards in front of me.

There was a crossroad junction right on the bend, which was mostly used by farm vehicles, and that day, some bugger decided to nip across the main road just as I was approaching. When I saw the nose of the tractor coming out, I instantly thought, Oh, shit! Brake. Then, within seconds, I noticed he had a trailer on the back, and I thought, Oh, shit! Brake harder!

My main focus was on the rear end of the trailer. If he decided to stall or stop at this point, I was almost certainly dead meat, because the car was still motoring on. My next thought as I was rapidly approaching collision, and all in a matter of seconds, was 'Fuck sake! Get the anchors on quick!' Now I was in lock-up and the car went into skid motion for sixty yards as I hit the bend and looked like hitting more than I wanted to.

When the point came where I was in eye contact with the tractor driver and still in a skid, by pure luck I cleared that trailer with inches to spare as the car kept skidding round the corner. Another sixty yards of skidding and I eventually began to regain control of the car. I glanced behind and saw the driver looking as though he had shit himself.

'Phew! That was lucky.' And I merrily continued on my way to that meeting of nothingness. Isn't fate a strange phenomenon? I made the meeting of nothingness, as expected, and got the request for more cash flows, as expected, and on the way home I slowed down at the Eagle Gates near Thankerton and saw my two lines of black tire tread gliding all the way round the corner. Colin McCrae, the late and great Scottish rally driver from Lanark, would have been impressed by such a skilful manoeuvre. I wasn't! It had nothing to do with skill, just pure luck. That would have been one helluva stupid and pointless way in which to depart dear old Mother Earth.

Back at the course, the tide was turning, but ever so slowly. People were appearing from all parts, not just the locals, and they would make promises of returning and possibly joining as members. What we didn't do was put on the hard sell and clinch those memberships there and then! The course was looking a picture and improved day by day. Keeping it that way was a constant struggle particularly as we were divorcing ourselves from it three or four days every week.

On each return visit, we would have to catch up with the sheep shit once more and get the greens cut for the weekend. This slipshod strategy was demoralising both of us, and even I could now see the writing that appeared to be on the wall.

July brought a brief moment of respite for Harry, Ross, and myself, when we took ourselves off to St Andrews for the Open Championship on one of the practice days. The practice days are the best time if you're hoping to make contact with the players or media. Sure enough, we had barely parked the car up and walked fifty yards when we bumped into Peter Alliss and the late Alex Hay taking a break from the commentary box.

Harry was in his element with this sort of thing, and they were duly given a glossy leaflet and a brief account of Arbory in the hope of getting a wee mention on the telly—and we did! After talking to them for ten minutes, we let them go and made for the action on the course. We were all wearing our hickory golf T-shirts, courtesy of the Glenmuir Knitwear Company which, at that time, was owned by our friend Malcolm Boyd from Biggar. The shirts worked a treat, because almost everybody who passed by scanned the logo to see what we were all about.

Around lunchtime, we encountered a bit of a fracas with a load of youngsters on the course. They were busy chasing Gary Player for his autograph, so we all joined in the chase. The wee bugger was still as fit as a fiddle for his encroaching years and made it easily to the safety of the spectator ropes and then began walking once inside them.

I called out to him, 'Hey, Gary! What do you think of this?' He turned round and looked at me from about thirty feet distance, and I threw a gutta ball right to his feet.

It was a vain attempt to attract his attention because he looked at the ball, then looked at the three of us and shouted back in his South African accent, 'It's a goota paircha—I can't accept gifts!' Then he threw the bloody ball straight back to me! I think you missed the point, Gary. Some you win, but we were losing far too many.

When we were browsing around the hospitality tents, we came across Butch Harmon, who was then Tiger Woods' coach. Harry, no messing, got right in there! And before we knew it, we were talking away like old pals. He was fascinated by our pitch, and we ended up giving him three of our best gutta balls. 'Get Tiger to give these a whack and see how far he can get them,' Harry buoyantly said to Butch.

'Gee, thanks. I will!' he replied and off he went.

We were told by some Americans a few days later that Tiger had indeed given those balls a whack with his modern metal Mickey and apparently managed 240 yards as his best, a feat which we never managed to confirm, but those same Yanks told us that they had seen us on American TV before they crossed the pond for The Open. Had the BBC managed to export some snippets of *Outside Now*?

Many other contacts were made though, including Sandy Lyle, who lived not far from Biggar back then; Jim Ackenback, the American sports writer; Tommy Horton; and our wee pal, Sandy Sinclair. Then, as we were getting ready to head home, we heard another cafuffle outside the front door of the R&A clubhouse and we went to investigate.

The scene was more akin to a rock festival with predominantly young girls screaming their heads off in anticipation of getting a young golfer's autograph. It was Per Ulrik Johannson of Sweden, whose father, Ove, we knew quite well as he had visited Arbory a while back and purchased some of our gutta balls for a Hickory event in Sweden.

There was no way we were going to be able to speak to him because he was being marshalled into an awaiting car to escape the admiring mob! Just as he was getting into the car, I shouted as loud as I could, 'Per Ulrik! Tell Ove we were asking for him!' He obviously heard me because he resisted the pushing and shoving of the marshals to get him safely into the car, as he frantically looked around at the madding crowd to see where that voice had came from. He succumbed to the pressures of the melee and was somewhat ungraciously whisked away to his hotel. Pity! And that brought an enjoyable day to a conclusion, and we all headed home to the awaiting reality of Arbory.

Harry would return to the Open the next day while I would get back to the course and get on with some shit pickin' and general maintenance tasks. It wasn't that long after the Open had finished and Mr Woods had lifted the Claret Jug that we received a Dragons' Den-like offer from our pals at *Bunkered Magazine*.

They had a pitch at the Open, where we'd told them about our cash flow problems and how we were struggling to survive in the world of golf. We hadn't thought much more of the conversation until Paul got in touch with Harry asking us to go into Glasgow and have a meeting with them.

We were also coming under pressure to make some sort of contribution towards our rent for the course. It was totally understandable, since the Hodge family had put in some considerable help with plant and materials, and after all, it was their ground we were squatting upon!

We went to see Duncan, and to his eternal credit, he must have noticed the concern on our faces at such a request, because he immediately put our minds at rest when he said, 'But we're not going to throw you off the ground if you can't come up with something!' We had a great deal to thank the Hodge family for, in our present circumstances of being totally skint!

The meeting in Glasgow with Paul, Steph, and Tom turned out to be an intriguing affair with a firm offer being laid on the table at the end of the day for us to consider! A big chunk of the finance lay in free advertising over the next five years, but what we desperately needed at this point in time was hard working cash. Another conflict of interest lay in the location of this hickory golf experience. Amazingly, they saw the future of the experience being located near Turnberry, on the west coast of Scotland.

Now there was good sound logic contained within such a suggestion, because Harry and I had often discussed the merits of being located nearer to one of Scotland's golfing hubs such as St Andrews or . . . Turnberry. But the reality was that we weren't a stone's throw away from one of these hubs; we were at Junction 13 of Scotland's busiest motorway, at which point the Edinburgh-bound travellers would fork off on their journey east. Glasgow, Edinburgh, and Carlisle were only a one-hour drive away.

The location was fine, if not ideal! Anyway, relocating the entire experience would mean wrenching ourselves away from the very soul of all our previous exploits and ambitions for the history of golf in Clydesdale. I, for one, wasn't prepared to discard our Arbory field with its hidden glut of hard manpower, working hours. Nah. Generous though the offer appeared, and it was certainly appreciated—we politely turned it down in the hope that the pendulum would finally swing in our favour, with Arbory paying her way.

People continued to come and go; it was just not enough of them and definitely not enough of them paying for the privilege! Various tour operators were popping in and making enthusiastic promises of sending business in the future. And tempers were fraying, both at home and at the course between Harry and me. Little wonder, because money was a rare commodity and both our families were suffering as a result.

The time had come when we were wishing we'd never started this bloody venture. I suppose I should be more grateful to the lottery winner and the few thousand that she ploughed into the business. It was barely enough to keep us afloat but just enough to retain a glimmer of hope. Perhaps we were being greedy. I would hate to think that greed could become the backbone of our enthusiasm!

We were fully learning and understanding the many warnings from business people that the vast majority of failed start-ups come from them being underfunded! It was all the more annoying when the lottery winner would boast that she and Robert could manage to live off their pension without touching the windfall. Oh aye, fuckin' marvellous achievement! She was in her eighties; just how long was she expecting to live? People being careful again. Why?

There was a major breakthrough on the maintenance front and, most particularly, the shit pickin' farce. We had been informed that a local farmer come farm plant salesman, John Gibson, owned a machine which he hired out to various agricultural shows and the like, for . . . shit pickin' the show fields before the events started!

Now this could be groundbreaking news for the back-breaking shit we were enduring. John agreed to bring his quad bike and sweeper machine up to the course and give us a demonstration on how to use it. The downside was crystal clear. We both knew we wouldn't be in any position to afford the hire of such a heaven-sent miracle of technology. But we had to see what this machine could do. Maybe one of us would get the lottery up, just like Audrey?

John arrived with the gear and promptly ran it off the trailer he was transporting it in. We made it absolutely clear to him that *the erse was hingin oot oor breeks*' and that we probably couldn't afford the hire at this time; he appeared to have a nonplussed attitude to the sad fact.

Suddenly, two wee boys had reappeared from the depths of despair at the sight of their possible salvation. John hooked the sweeper on to the quad and kicked them both up, then started running up and down the fifth fairway (what fairway?) which was generally one of the dirtiest parts of the course. The impact was immediate, as before our eyes we could see our wee course being effectively hoovered clean. Not only was the shit being brushed up, but all the wee bits of wool and moss too! This was our biggest discovery since Graham had sourced the gutta-percha.

What happens now? We re-emphasised our state of poverty while telling John that this was definitely the machine of our dreams! 'Look,' he said, 'I'll leave both the quad and the sweeper with you, and you can try them out until the weekend. I won't be hard on you. All the shows are finished now, and I don't have any hires for it now anyway.'

John was another one of the good guys. He could see what his machine meant to us, and his heart was probably telling him that here were two guys who needed a wee break of some sort. It was in his power to yield a wee hand of support—and he did.

The next few days relieved some of the frustrations as we almost fought for the rights to the quad and sweeper. This was bloody marvellous and an insight into how much more easier life could be with the aid of a machine here and there. Within two days of working the sweeper, the entire course had taken a completely new look. A look that said, 'Look at me. *I really am* a golf course. Come and play me.'

Strange to think of it, but, nobody in the world had ever seen this small piece of ground in its present condition of pristine beauty! However, there were even better advantages to be gained from our temporary use of this modern mechanical gadgetry. It took all of five seconds to unhook the sweeper, and then we had instant taxi service to every corner of the course. We were in heaven, but it wouldn't last!

Another film crew came from Pilot TV and spent a couple of hours filming on the course. What they did and said I've never known or if it was ever aired on the telly. But they left fifty quid for the privilege, and that went to John when he came to pick up his quad and sweeper. Life was ambling away in the slow lane of prosperity and out of control in regard to activity.

I embarked on a spurious campaign of lettering anybody and everybody linked to Scottish tourism and that kiddie-on parliament at Holyrood. We'd already received a disgusting knock-back from the blazers at the Royal & Ancient after we tried them for some funding assistance. They disperse millions in funding every year all around the globe. Their letter of rejection was an insult and lacked any form of graciousness or content as to why we were so much out of favour. I didn't miss them with my response! Oh, the rascals!

Archie phoned Harry to ask if we could play in the England v Scotland hickory golf match at Alnmouth, and we decided to give a go. Harry was attired as the typical artisan and I the crabbit-looking meenister. Apart from the three-hour hike to get there, it turned out to be a really fun day with Harry and I winning our match, but Scotland losing overall. Buggers! Only joking.

It was good to see Archie again along with the other Golf Collectors Society members, and our appearance went down well with the healthy crowd who had gathered to watch the matches tee off. Back at Arbory, our pal Stevie Callan shot a record 35 over Arbory, albeit with the easier gutty ball. And then we had two Canadians accompanied by their wives play the course. Rather ironically, they were all in agreement that their experience had been a fantastic bonus to their Scottish trip. One of the wives added, 'This beats St Andrews!'

One day, I had an unusual experience while walking along the top of the course near the third green. It was a typical autumnal day with frequent showers and sunny intervals. They say you'll never find the end of a rainbow—but I did! I wish Harry had been there to witness this illusion too. Obviously, it was pissing down, and there in front of me and overhead spanned a beautiful rainbow crossing to the other side of the river Clyde, perhaps a mile away.

As I traced the rainbow's arc from the Clyde, and over my head to the bottom of Arbory Hill, I honestly couldn't believe my eyes. There it was, only forty feet away to my right. Perhaps this was an omen, I was thinking. I was a bit weary, but certainly not drunk or under the influence of any drugs. So confounded by the clarity of my vision, I even thought about taking a wee walk over to the fence line to where it, apparently, ended. Nah?

My fatigued legs were telling me not to be so bloody stupid and spare my diminishing energy for getting to the third green where I was working. I think God was having a wee laugh at my expense and I wasn't for giving him the satisfaction. The bugger!

Winter was just round the corner, and that meant some serious winter maintenance of the greens—feather raking the greens to get the moss removed, tining to aereate them, then top dressing and giving them a feed to see them through the winter ahead. All this was seriously hard graft with simple hand tools and a wheel barrow. It was truly authentic restoration work, just as Old Tom and Honeyman would have toiled, except they would have the luxury of a horse and cart.

Worst of all was the top dressing which we had to hand-barrow to the greens, mostly uphill, because we simply didn't have any machinery to make the task so much easier. This was pure madness and the craziest form of assisted suicide.

Being a couple of business numpties, we joined an entrepreneurial programme held at East Kilbride on the south side of Glasgow. The programme offered help with all aspects of business start-up, including accountancy, sales and marketing, legal advice, etc. What harm could it do, and Ewan, the programme organiser, had let us in on a two-for-one deal. We would milk it for all we could, and it was no loss to attend once a week during the dark winter evenings.

One of Harry's contacts appeared in September for a meeting at the course, a smashing guy by the name of Frazer Blyth, who was working as a marketing manager for a new gift experience company called Boondoggle. On one occasion, Harry set up a table and three chairs chairs on the eighth tee, and we sat and had a meeting bathed in warm sunshine. These businesses were beginning to pop up thanks to the incredible World Wide Web and the Internet coming to the fore. Timing again? Oh, how we could have benefitted from the Internet technology being more advanced at the time of our start-up.

Frazer was shown round the course, and the experience explained to him over a cup of tea. When asked what he thought of the place, he almost infected us with 'his' enthusiasm for hickory golf. He went on to tell us quite emphatically that he would be amazed if the experience didn't sell, and sell well! Hope springs eternal, and Frazer could just be the answer to all our prayers. There was no point in relying upon the Big Man to help—he's just not reliable. I was beginning to think he was a bit of a . . . rascal?

The saga continued, and we managed to complete the maintenance on the greens by the end of October. With no money coming in, I continued to take on work with Ronnie, and he helped with various bits and bobs in the pavilion. We did manage to sell a few gutta balls but not in significant enough numbers to allow any cause for celebration. And those futile meetings with Scottish Enterprise and our local council continued to drum up . . . absolutely nothing!

Those people we were having to deal with were the gatekeepers who had the power to unlock the doors of funding opportunities. You just had to read a few business newspapers to see where some of the dosh was being squandered and not the ten grand lump sums we were chasing. Oh no! Try £500,000 as an example!

The solitary positive heading towards Christmas was the encouragement we received from Ewan at the entrepreneurial programme and the lessons being learnt there. For what practical reason, I really didn't know. Ewan never ceased to lavish praise upon our business idea, but *he* wasn't a gatekeeper.

Harry had managed to procure two excellent endorsements of the project. The first was from Ben Crenshaw, a great golfer, golf course architect, and lover of golf history, which included a picture of Ben for use in our leaflets and brochures. The second was from the Duke of York, who wished us every success with the venture and who, somewhat ironically, became captain of the R&A golf club?

In working together, we had a lot going for us. I was good at some things, and Harry was good at other things. Unfortunately, the one critical thing we were both hopeless at was selling! It doesn't matter how much hard graft you put into your product and how good it is—if you can't sell it, it's useless.

Then at the start of December there were reports in the papers that a company was struggling and about to fold. Yes, it was Boondoggle! What next? Why was this misfortune continually happening to us?

Harry kept in touch with Frazer, and after only a fortnight of Boondoggle going down, there was a tiny sparkle of light in our crestfallen tunnel of golfing enterprise. Frazer had been recruited in the management team of the Red Letter Days' gift experience company, which was owned at that time by Rachel Elnaugh. He remained fully on board and was committed to promoting hickory golf, every bit as confident in selling the experience for his new employers.

The downside to all this was that time was not on our side. Setting up a new relationship with Red Letter Days wasn't going to happen overnight, and if they did manage to sell the experience on our behalf, those customers wouldn't be appearing any time soon.

Happy New Year!

Dreams, Disinfectant, and Compensation

Considering everything that had occurred prior to 2001, in relation to our broken dream, it was vital that we now make some sort of positive impression to get some cash in the kitty and get that dream back on track. Although it was only January, the clock was ticking, and the odds of survival were stacking up against us.

The course was in fantastic condition but with little chance of seeing any touring golfers as early as this. It gave us the opportunity of continuing with promotional work and chasing those illusive funders of enterprise. I had a holiday coming up in February and would be back at the start of March with high hopes of a change in our fortunes for the better.

We continued to purge golf magazines and the web for golfing email contacts, and we were building up quite a considerable database—for all it was worth! For every block of 100 emails sent out touting our wares, we were lucky if we received one reply. UK and Irish golf clubs, individuals from various golfing societies, and anything with a connection to golf made our list. It was obviously and greatly disappointing to us; these emails were finding the delete button faster than you could say, 'Gie us a break!' Endless hours of tedium for absolutely nothing.

It was while I was still on that holiday that the first rumblings were being made of a possible outbreak of foot-and-mouth disease in the United Kingdom. If this turned out to be true, nobody could have written this script, because I remembered the disastrous consequences of the last outbreak in 1967. I knew immediately that this could be the final straw, especially as our business was located in a completely rural setting with grazing sheep playing an integral part of the course maintenance!

It was true, and by early March, restrictions on access to the countryside were already in place, which meant that Arbory Braes was declared 'out of bounds' for both visitors and the two-man management team. This was simply unacceptable, because Mother Nature had been in abeyance for the winter months, and she was almost ready to come out of her winter hibernation and reap havoc on our wee golf course! Maybe we were just stuck in a horrible nightmare and we would wake up soon? . . . Nope!

Duncan eventually gave in to our pleas for access to the ground in April so long as we followed the disinfectant code for entering farm property. This entailed dipping your boots in a tray of expensive soapy water! That cost us fifty quid for disinfectant from the local vet, where a bottle of Fairy Liquid would have done the same job for pennies.

To make matters even worse, our first visit to the course in almost two months revealed that we'd incurred a break-in in one of the kabins. Some dirty bastard had broken in and stolen the generator that we'd bought from Ronnie. The hangin' judge from Dundee was right when he said a couple of hundred years ago, '*Hing a thief when he's young, and he'll no steal when he's auld!*'

Life was proving to be a pure bitch, but there were a few positives coming out of the woodwork at the same time. Harry had been making some great contacts through the Scottish Tourism Board, and we attended a trade fair in Glasgow. Everybody we talked to were enthralled with the hickory golf concept, and Frazer had signed us up to the red-letter day's list of experiences and they were beginning to sell hickory golf to their customers. Hey ho! The sun might just shine again.

I was also busy writing to anybody and everybody. I was getting a few letters published in *The Scotsman* broadsheet, protesting against the inept handling of the foot-and-mouth crisis as well as giving a few members of the Scottish (kiddie-on) Parliament a piece of my mind. In golf, I decided to send a letter to the legendary Jack Nicklaus and included a few gutta balls. Pity, he never bothered to respond.

The sky hadn't fallen in yet—but it was getting close. A few enquiries continued to trickle in for memberships and packages, and we had to hope that such interest would remain patient and wait for this latest crap to pass over. Three funding possibilities were being pursued through Scottish Enterprise, but we wouldn't be holding our breath on those.

On the financial side, we managed to secure a £10,000 overdraft facility on our account to keep us going, which was guaranteed by my mother-in-law. You know, the lady with a million in the same bank! We also had to try and sort out a few legal aspects of the business with our local lawyer, John Armstrong. John had given us legal counsel on a couple of occasions now and hadn't taken a single penny for his service. 'I'll come knocking your door when the money starts rolling in,' he said. Another one of the good guys!

While I was repairing the dyke in our car park one day, a wee collie dug appeared on the scene from out of the blue. I immediately befriended 'dug' while asking anyone who passed by if they knew who he belonged to. Nobody knew 'dug', so I shared my sandwich with him at lunchtime and he followed my every step all day.

My thoughts meandered back to when I was about fourteen and had trained Shane, Grace's Irish setter, to find golf balls. And find them he did, much to the annoyance of some of the golfers when they saw me heading home sporting a bag full of . . . their golf balls.

What a dog, and what a joy to watch him at work! Maybe I could train 'dug' to chase those bloody sheep up the hill when we didn't want them on the course.

When it came time to go home, I said my goodbyes to 'dug', but the little bugger decided to park himself near the front wheels of the car. I think he was trying to tell me something, but he wasn't mine to take away. I opened the passenger side door and let him into the car and took him down to the local bobby in the village, for all the good that it did. The polis weren't in the least bit interested in lost dogs and still hadn't found the bastard who stole the Genny either!

I decided to take him home and reluctantly phoned the farm to see if Duncan knew who he belonged to, but I was now hoping that 'dug' was my new-found friend and companion. No such luck! Dug had escaped from captivity in the farm shed he was kept in, and the young herd who had lost him was on his way to Biggar to take him home. Shit! And talking of shit, he had got a good feed before the herd came to collect him, and he managed to shit on the kitchen floor before departing forever. Awww! And that was the end of 'dug'.

It was the middle of May and we were still stranded in the middle of the foot-and-mouth travesty, and tempers were fraying with the frustration of it all. Harry and I were sitting in the pavilion having ineffectually washed our boots in disinfectant as was the required procedural sham, when the phone rang. It was someone from the Abington hotel informing us that they had three people in the lobby enquiring about the golf course and wanting to come over to see it. Harry took the call and relayed the conversation to me.

'It's a Mr and Mrs Morris from America and a Scottish friend wanting to come over,' he said.

I shook my head and said, 'Ach. We cannae let them near the place, Harry.'

'They've come down from Dornoch to see us.'

'Dornoch!' I exclaimed. 'Bloody hell, what a hike!' And I shook my head again.

Harry looked at me and said, 'I think we should go over to the hotel and meet them.'

'Aye, you're right. That's the least we can do. Tell them we'll be over in five minutes.'

So we made our way over to the hotel and met up with the three of them where we explained the extraordinary circumstances we were embroiled in. After about twenty minutes of dialogue and apology, Harry pulled me to the side and whispered, 'Let's take them ower tae the course. What harm is it going to do?'

Yet another shake of the head, and I thought, Why not? 'Aye. Let's take them over in our car, and you can tell them to leave their car here. Let's hope Duncan or George don't go by or there could be a rammy!' The restrictions were a farce, but they were legally binding. Various scientists were publicly saying as much.

Harry explained the plan of attack, and Mr Morris asked, 'Are you sure? We don't want you to get into trouble, just for us.' Harry assured him that it would be OK, and we drove them over to the pavilion. As we turned round the corner at the caravan park, Duncan's hand-painted sign in dripping blood red greeted us as we neared the course—KEEP OUT! It was kind of effective and scary that sign, and I don't think many ignored it, with the exception of thieves, of course.

It was reminiscent of Clint Eastwood's sign in one of his cowboy movies. When we got to the pavilion, the first thing we had to do was to make them all paddle through the disinfectant tray before going into the pavilion, with Harry and I squinting over our shoulder to see if anybody else was going about.

Once in the pavilion, Harry and I 'went into one', talking our way through all the photos on the walls and showing them as much as we could of the course from the sanctity of the big glass window inside the pavilion. Somehow I just knew that Harry was going to suggest taking them up on to the course for a look-see at the top of the first hole. 'Alfie, why don't we take a quick jaunt up the first? Nobody can see very much from down here,' he said.

Harry was obviously quite relaxed with the situation, but I was as nervous as hell. Once more I succumbed to the request, and we all headed up the first hole to the top of the course. I can remember saying to them as we started to ascend the first hillock, 'Now don't look back till we get to the top!' Five minutes later, we were at the top of the course, and I said to them, 'OK. You can turn round now.'

To which, Mr Morris's reaction was a simple 'Wow!'

'Was that a wow I heard there?' I asked.

'Wow, wow, wow!' he reaffirmed.

We began describing the layout of the holes and the names of the surrounding hills. It was a lovely clear sunny day, and Tinto was clearly visible in the distance. We would also be clearly visible to prying eyes from the village just across the Clyde, and so I called a halt to proceedings and we all walked back down to the privacy of the pavilion.

Tea and coffee were served and the gutta ball described in detail while taking a photo of Tom sitting in front of his famous namesake, Tom Morris of St Andrews. We didn't have much to sell apart from some guttas, and two were purchased prior to winding up the visit and returning them back to the hotel.

There was a bit of mumbling going on between Mr and Mrs Morris, and then Tom produced his wallet and started to leaf out a couple of twenty pound notes. 'We'd like to give you something for your time, boys.' Harry immediately declined the offer with some back-up from me. But they were adamant to part with their money, and it was funny to see Mrs Morris giving Tom a discreet dig in the ribs. As he leafed out another twenty, he got another dig. Then another twenty and another dig, until he had £100 in his hands which he forced into Harry's hand.

Another day, another dollar? A hundred quid for a walk in the park! The Morrises were lovely and generous people who didn't get much for their dollar that day. Harry took them back over to the hotel where they drove to Edinburgh to continue their holiday. Tom phoned Harry later that day to thank us for allowing them to see the course, and he informed Harry that Mrs Morris was crying when they left Abington.

Time was rolling on, and a few potential customers continued to brave Duncan's blood-red 'Keep Out' sign only to be told that we couldn't allow them to play the course because of the restrictions. No doubt there were others whom we missed on the days when we weren't at the course.

The Hodges were still reluctant to let the public have access due to all the uncertainty surrounding the entire shambles. Nobody knew a bloody thing about anything! It was perfectly clear that the government ministries for agriculture had learnt absolutely nothing from the 1967 outbreak. A complete and utter disgrace!

I started trying to chase up some of the compensation on offer for lost business income. I was given an Edinburgh phone number (0131 666 879) to enquire about how to get some of that cash. The girl who answered my call informed me that I had the wrong number and gave me another in the same building. I tried that—and they didn't handle compensation either, and they gave me another number. Again, I tried that with the same result but once again got a very helpful additional number.

My piece of A4 paper was beginning to look like a clock face as I wrote each number down. Six times I phoned and six times I was hedged to another obscure department. I was starting to wonder if any of these people actually knew that foot-and-mouth disease had been causing havoc in the United Kingdom for the past five months. Oh well! Another number followed and I wrote it down on the piece of paper and hung up the phone. Just as I was about to try again, I glanced at the first number at the top of the page—0131 666 879. Life's a cycle. Bastards!

Another minute of fame was realised when Lanarkshire TV asked us to do a live gig at their studio in Shotts. Although the interview went really well with both of us handling the 'live' questioning unerringly, I wasn't too happy about this *live* carry-on. Back at the course, John Gibson returned with his quad bike and sweeper and told us we could use them as much as we wanted. When we told him we couldn't afford the hire, he simply shrugged his shoulders and told us he wasn't expecting any hires because all the agricultural shows had now been cancelled due to the restrictions, and then he said we could have it for nothing. In John, we had found a real gem of a guy, and we took full advantage of his generosity in the hope that we would be in a position to pay him back some day—just like John Armstrong and the Hodges.

As the months rolled by, the countryside evoked an unusual surreal landscape of somewhat unnatural colour, with barren fields bereft of livestock. Herds and flocks that had been culled left empty and un-grazed fields, which in turn produced swathes of untouched wild flora, predominantly buttercups, displaying acre upon acre of undulating yellow blankets.

Like wars, a foot-and-mouth epidemic is a dirty business with unscrupulous people trying to make gain from a national disaster. Government compensation handouts were outrageously generous, giving rise to rumours that some farmers would be quite happy to have their own livestock infected!

In an agricultural climate which necessitated the importance of being careful, a few were trying *not* to be careful. Big bucks were to be made from the culling operation and the consequent clean-up of the carcases. The whole thing was unquestionably a disaster—but also a total farce.

At one point there were reports that some of the slaughter men engaged in the task of culling the animals were in need of counselling. For Christ's sake! Gory as it may seem, the task in hand was actually those people's day-to-day profession, and they were earning the best money they could ever expect to get from it. Makes you kinda wonder if grave diggers get some form of counselling during *their* working careers.

And then there were the contractors who hired out their plant for the cause. Some bought brand-new machines and had them paid off in a couple of months work. Although the doomed animals didn't lie around long enough to make a stink, everything else connected with foot-and-mouth disease certainly did stink!

I remember having a discussion with Duncan and his father, George, about the possibilities of them making some fast cash by hiring their own plant and machinery and being told without hesitation that they had no intention of getting involved in other people's misery! I admired their attitude that it just didn't seem right to make gain from such a situation.

At the start of August, the confusion continued with the fishers being allowed back on to the Clyde to fish—provided the farmers were happy to let them cross over their land. We kept niggling away at Duncan, in a very subtle manner, to allow us to open up for business. He finally succumbed on 10 August, and we could now tell the golfing world that we were now open for business.

We decided to hold an open day at the end of the month, but only a dozen turned up. What we desperately needed was a miraculous floodgate to be opened up and the customers to come flooding in, just like the ending to the film—*Field of Dreams*. That was being optimistic in the extreme, and the reality was that only a few customers played the course over the first month of opening.

But the sun was shining again, and we received a good booking for twelve Americans on 10 September, who would be touring Scotland's golf courses, and they wanted to make a visit on 21 September. Rockin' an' rollin' at last? Well, that's what we thought, but we forgot that somebody else was writing this script.

The 9/11 atrocity took place, and that booking was cancelled on 13 September by email! The American golfer was one of our main targets for winning custom, but their confidence in flying had been understandably shattered, and many were cancelling their trips to Scotland through their tour operators.

There was one day, when I was chatting to a customer just outside the pavilion, that I spotted a fox sauntering down the hill in the distance. As it got closer, I brought it to the attention of the customer. 'Oh, look! Here comes Mr Fox to see you,' I said excitedly. We stood there motionless and silent as it got nearer and nearer, prancing down the hill with a gallus strut until it stood only a few yards away from us at the bottom side of the seventh green. With a right brazen look, he stopped and glared over at us for a few moments before carrying on to the fields adjacent to the course. We looked at each other and had a bit of a laugh at the pure display of cheek we had just witnessed and then carried on with our conversation.

Barely ten minutes later, there he was again, returning from his hunting mission, and this time with a freshly caught rabbit in his mouth. Once more, the bugger retraced his same path on the return journey and stopped at the same spot, dropped the rabbit, and looked at us as if to say, 'What the bloody hell are you twa lookin at?' Then he picked up the rabbit and made off back up the hill with that same gallus strut! Such moments were precious!

And then there was Mr and Mrs Stoat who had decided to take free lodgings under the floor of our pavilion! We didn't actually know this until we detected a stale smell inside the pavilion one day and couldn't for the life of us work out where that odious pong was coming from. It turned out that the stoats were getting into the foundations through a small hole I had failed to seal off when we built the drains for the toilet and kitchen.

The smell was that of a dead rabbit, and the stoats were thereby evicted, making sure they weren't trapped inside before sealing up the hole. Anyway, they were a regular feature darting in and out, up and down on the nearby drystane dyke only a few yards from the pavilion.

Stoats are gorgeous creatures, but as wild as you get! One day, Harry and I were inside the pavilion and came out for a look around when there, right in front us, about seven yards away, was Mr Stoat with his dinner, a young rabbit, in his mouth. He was immediately startled by our presence and dropped the dead rabbit and scampered into some clumps of rushes nearby.

Sensing an opportunity in the making, I went into the pavilion and got the camcorder ready for a possible David Attenborough moment. I rejoined Harry outside, and we stood like statues in anticipation of the stoat reappearing from the rushes. 'Dae ye think he'll come out when we're here, Alfie?'

'Ah dinnae ken. But ah wouldna leave ma dinner there for somebody else to steal!'

Sure enough, he started to peek out from the rushes, rather concerned about the well-being of his dinner. This was going to be a game of cat and mouse, or perhaps Harry and stoat, over the next few minutes. Well, it took a bit longer and a lot of patience from us, but ever so slowly, the stoat got braver and braver till he was nearly back to within biting distance of his lunch. We were whispering all the time, and I said to Harry, 'Try and get a bit closer to the rabbit.'

When Harry took a couple of steps towards the rabbit, the stoat took off and hid back in the rushes. But he must have been hungry, because he didn't wait too long before coming back out and made another try for the rabbit. Harry then nudged himself nearer and nearer till his boots were almost touching the rabbit, and Mr Stoat was watching his every movement.

I was busy taking the footage and was praying that the bloody battery didn't go flat on me! This was fascinating. After a wee while, the stoat became confident enough to try and drag the rabbit away from Harry's feet, at which point Harry bent over and put his hand, complete with five fingers, pointing next to the rabbit and the stoat. I whispered to Harry a precautionary warning, 'Ah wouldna dae that, Harry. He'll huv yer bloody finger aff in a jiffy!' At which he promptly withdrew his hand.

Eventually, we both withdrew and allowed Mr Stoat to drag off his prey before it went past the sell-by date. What an encounter with raw nature! Not long after this, we noticed them over at the first tee next to the dyke, but there weren't just the two stoats; there were five or six!

Mr and Mrs had obviously been busy, and the young stoats were jumping and somersaulting all over the place, apparently, practising for a kill of their own some day. One them must have noticed us standing behind the big glass window and decided to come over and say hello. As we stood there watching, it pranced over to the bench seat directly under the window and jumped up on to it, then stood up on its hind legs using the window sill to lean on . . . and peered back into the window at us! 'What are you two looking at? Never seen a stoat before?' Isn't nature so bloody marvellous!

Building this experience wasn't a problem in the slightest—but selling it was. If only we'd had the benefit of the *Dragon's Den* TV programme, then we might have better understood some of the nitty-gritty procedures of business issues They do say that you can have the best business idea in the world—but if you can't sell it, then it's useless! Then again, it had been a rather bumpy ride with so much going against us.

Harry had come to the end of his tether, and all this never-ending hassle had taken its toll. Tell me about it; the shit was hitting the fan everywhere! He told me he was packing it in and duly resigned and left the business at the end of September.

How could I blame him? We were jinxed by the laws of circumstance and luck. I had to think long and hard about coming to the same decision myself. In hindsight, I should have tried to iron things out with him and find some solution. But I found out much later that there had been another influence behind his decision. Another winter was on the doorstep, which meant that I could step back from the course and do some paid work with Ronnie.

The winter itinerary was well established by now. Just keep on top of the course, as and when I could, make a pound here and there, and promote on the Internet during the long winter nights. Aye, decision made! We *had* built it—and the people *were* beginning to come! I just had to give this business one more throw of the dice. You can't do all this hard work without something good coming of it, can you?

The month ended well, considering I was now a solitary figure trudging a lonesome path to one of two possible outcomes—success or failure. There were loads of things going on, positive things! Albert Sangenis, a friend in Spain, had a couple of articles published, and Scottish Enterprise had actually assisted by doing a press run in local newspapers which covered the entire south of Scotland area.

Mike Graf, a tour operator, had come to see me at the course and promised to try and sell the experience at a trade fair he was attending in Germany. I also had enquiries and a few small bookings coming in all the time, and heaven knows who else was writing about hickory golf in magazines and newspapers. Red Letter Days had sent two young lads to sample our wares before Harry's resignation and were now ready to go with a big promotional slot in the *Daily Record* newspaper. What scared me most was the £75 price tag they'd put on the experience. My cut was £50, but that included a three course lunch at Toby's small restaurant in the village.

On the playing front, I'd received an enquiry from a fourball from Edinburgh who had purchased a Boondoggle package before they went down. Naturally, I told them I would honour the package, but I couldn't feed them as well. They came in October and had a great day out and left a £40 bung in the visitors' book for me to find.

About the same time, I had a visit from Peter Craigon and three of his pals from the Stirling area to play a game of hickory for charity. They would raise £2000 for their charity, which confirmed our open door policy of embracing similar events in the future.

Just before Christmas, there was an article in the paper whereby London lawyers urged Scottish businesses to sue the government for the foot-and-mouth debacle. I had wasted far too much time and energy on the dirty issue to be bothered with any more attempts for compensation. I wasn't a farmer, a hotel or B&B operator, so my face didn't fit the handout regime!

I asked my friends Pete and Margaret who ran a small B&B in Biggar if they had tried for compensation. They had and actually got something. But Pete told me that they hadn't been that badly affected as their numbers weren't down all that much! I'd learnt so much crap about matters that had no relevance to golf courses all over the country—except mine of course. Then, just to rub salt into the wounds, one government official asked me why our golf course was closed to the public in the first place. Dahhhh!

What a year, and not even close to getting a penny in compensation. The funders I was aimlessly chasing had been given a foot-and-mouth out clause which suited their agenda. 'Oh dear. We can't do much to help you while you're not trading.'

Maybe Lady Luck will finally throw some good fortune my way for the last throw of the dice in the New Year?

Ever the optimist.

Stars, Pros, Saints, and Sinners

2002 was going to be a crunch year for the business. It didn't take a brain surgeon to work that one out! But amazingly, it was starting to throw up threads of hope when in late spring I had not one, not two, but three very interesting developments. The first was an email from Robert Harris, the director of golf at The Greenbrier in the States. I never got to the bottom of how they knew about Arbory, but I had a rough idea based upon my intellectual prowess.

The Greenbrier was the golfing home of the great Sam Snead, who should require no introduction regarding his golfing curriculum vitae. Sam had a good friend, Lewis Keller, who owned the historic Oakhurst Links only a few miles from The Greenbrier Resort. Oakhurst turned out to be a slight pain in the backside to us because Lewis, with some help from Sam, set up the first authentic hickory golf links in America where the nine hole course there dated back to 1884.

As a result, we couldn't really tout ourselves as being the first in the world at Arbory, so they stole our thunder on that little issue—we were, however, the first in *the home of golf!* Anyway, Robert emailed me to say that they intended to send over to me a hickory club autographed by Sam himself! Not only that, Sam would go out and hit a ball with this club, and they would take a photograph to authenticate this fantastic gesture of goodwill. Well, bugger me! And all this was going to happen after Sam had returned from The Masters opening ceremony at Augusta, where he traditionally struck the first ball of the tournament. OK, fine.

The second straw of hope came when at the end of April I received another email, this time from a *London Telegraph* journalist by the name of John Gibb. John wanted to write up an article describing a modern-day professional playing the course and for which he had Scotland's very own Open winner Paul Lawrie in mind.

Paul was probably the only ever winner of this prestigious tournament who (shamefully) never got the true credit he deserved for winning it! Well, bugger me again. Maybe 2002 would be the year after all to prove the visionless bastards wrong? John would keep me updated on who he would get and when we would be in a position to set this one up.

And finally, the third contact came a bit later in the year about mid-July. Some unknown golf writer from the States emailed me to ask if he could play the course sometime in the summer with a view to writing an article for *Golf Magazine* in America. His name was James Dodson, and I told him he would be made most welcome whenever he decided to come to Arbory.

I had been working my socks off since January with some welcome help from my son, Ross. I don't know what I would have done without him since Harry had thrown in the towel. Everything was coming together great and the course just needed Mother Nature to green her up a wee bit, while the pavilion was all that it should be, considering the lack of funds. I was working with Ronnie most of the time and gave the course as much time as I possibly could, which was fine for this non-growing time of the year.

That workload policy just wouldn't stack up once Arbory decided to come alive again and especially since I was expecting to be working with Ronnie from March onwards on the provision that my course and customers came first, if I had any.

I had managed to sell a miserable twelve vouchers over the Christmas period and that certainly wasn't going to be enough to survive. The Red Letter Days people were having more success, and they told me they'd sold around a hundred vouchers to their customers. To me, that was worth about £5,000 which was brilliant, but I had to fill in the gaps, somehow, or I was done for!

At nights, I would send out hundreds of emails and post some leaflets to selective possibilities and do any administration tasks like filing a tax return for the accountant, a really good guy, David Stimpson, from whom I got help through the entrepreneurial programme I was with. Hell, I did that through a March evening till five thirty in the morning before falling asleep on the chair, then went out with Ronnie at eight! Lunacy or what?

I also spent extensive hours on the signs being made by Pro Sports, the guys who offered us free advertising and a capital sum for 50 per cent of the company. There would be one big A0 sign at each tee, giving a blend of some general and local golf history.

I had to get these sorted out because it was the only funding help I was going to get from the public coffers in Scottish Enterprise! Countless and wasted hours were spent on the mathematical lies that are called cash flow projections! I came to the conclusion that the bigger the lies you told, the better chance you had of receiving some form of funding. I never did like liars!

Along with my promotional efforts, I was busy sending out irate pleas to local and national politicians seeking urgent assistance to keep my Titanic dream afloat. One, a Scottish tourism minister, was too busy trying to set fire to a hotel! What fuckin' chance could I really expect to have from these creepy crawlies of Scottish politics? And me an openly self-confessed nationalist—and proud of it too!

The sky was definitely falling in! Auld Aud gave a lifeline input of funds which basically went to propping up my own ailing bank account by virtue of a meagre wage from the course. There was also growing pressure on my abstinence in paying any form of lease to the Hodges. I could hardly complain, could I?

We'd had courtesy of the land all this time and paid next to nothing for the privilege. I did manage to do some building work for them at the farms they owned which helped to counter their old adage that 'everything has tae pay fur itself!' No argument there.

During the first months up to April, I was getting people calling in from time to time for a look around, and most of them would promise to return some day for a game. A few did have a game when the course was free of any snow while a few others got their freebie promotional games. But then there would be the ones whom I'd missed completely because I wasn't at the course full-time. Shit happens, and the future only looked bleaker with the summer months and the growing season approaching fast!

I got another email from Robert Harris saying that the club was definitely coming my way as soon as they could pin Sam down, and I started telling everyone I met about this little coup. Sam would regularly quote some of the wisest words to golfers seeking tips: *'Practice puts brains in your muscles!'* The Masters was on the telly, which is a must see for me every year—*The* Masters and *The* Open! If I see them, I'm happy. Please note that it is *the* Open—no such thing as the British Open!

But The Masters at glorious Augusta had a special significance this year, didn't it? I hadn't bothered too much about the opening ceremony before, but I just had to make sure I saw Slammin' Sam Snead do his stuff this year, if the Beeb actually showed it. They did, and unfortunately for Sam, he mishit that opening shot into the adoring crowd lining the first fairway (yes, fairway) and . . . bonk!

Some poor guy took a sore one on the nut, and apparently, Sam was quite upset about it. Beautiful, gorgeous Augusta—manicured to the point of insane precision. Absolutely beautiful! Pity it's being ruined by two ineffective ruling bodies.

I never thought any more of the incident until The Masters was over and reports were being made with regards to Sam's health. Sadly, Sam died on 24 May 2002. Gone was one of the world's greatest golfing legends, and gone too were my hopes of getting that club!

He had never recovered his health on returning from Augusta, and therefore his wonderful gesture to me was never fulfilled. I received a response to an email I had sent to Robert Harris at The Greenbrier stating: *'Now you know why we didn't manage to get the club to you as promised.'* How many can say that a true gentleman and legend of golf had gone and died on them? RIP, Mr Samuel Snead.

Staying on the American theme, another test for the project came in early May with a group of eleven Americans on their way to Turnberry. They had booked the experience through their tour operator, Sam Baker, and this would serve as a good learning curve for me in handling a group of players as opposed to the singles and fourballs which had become the norm.

Like the Americans that they were, they arrived at 100 miles per hour and left at just about the same speed! They were a fantastic bunch of professional people (doctors and surgeons, I think), and my wife, Dorothy, and daughter, Kelly, helped with the modest spread of sandwiches, tea, coffee, and whisky that we'd put on for them.

They obviously loved it. For them, it was a blast! I just wished that they'd taken more time to enjoy their unique taste of Scottish golf history—in the slow lane! But that's just the way the Yanks do things when they come to play golf in the homeland—fast and furious. Arbory at nine and Turnberry at half past . . . nine! A quick lunch, then maybe Carnoustie at one before going on to Royal Dornoch in the Highlands for teatime.

Ah jeest love these people but with no sexual connotations. One member of the party in particular, Paul Lavaroni, kept in touch for a while through email and never stopped praising the experience. Neil Hunter had appeared at the course during their visit and came to the exact same conclusion as myself that they were all people in a hurry! *Never hurry, never worry, and don't forget to smell the flowers along the way.* So true, Mr Hagen, but perhaps you should tell your compatriots?

When they'd finished their nine hole sprint, they got tucked into that spread we'd laid on, and by Christ, they didn't half tuck in! There wasn't a crumb left for the hungry proprietor, since I would normally act as scavenger to any leftovers. This day I was left hungry but satisfied beyond belief!

Just another instance when the people vindicated our belief in a non-rip-off experience. As they all departed the pavilion to take their seats on the awaiting bus, each and every one offered a strong handshake which is customary and polite for us golfers. And with some relief to my wracked body, they took themselves off for their next sojourn to Turnberry and the best golf course I've ever played in my lifetime, Turnberry Ailsa!

Neil was saying his goodbyes too to his newly discovered friends in golf and came into the pavilion just as I was reflecting in the restored quiet and tranquillity—I really needed Harry to share in such workloads even though they were stimulating and fun. But he wasn't there any more.

And then, just as I was beginning to retreat into one of those fucking depressions, Sam Baker strode into the pavilion where Neil and I had just sat down.

'Alfie!' he shouted. 'The guys want to see you in the bus for one last request. Could you come with me please?'

'Aye. Of course, I will, Sam. Is there a problem?' I asked.

'Oh no. They just want you to sign their scorecards and say a final farewell.'

'Oh right. We'd better do it then, Sam.'

We walked out to the car park, and I climbed into the bus where they were all waiting. And then there began an impatient clamour of scorecards waving in claustrophobic air space, ever hopeful of an obscure scribble from an even more obscure human being. Fuck me! This was my first fan club! As I wrote, I grew strangely sombre with joy because I'd never really thought about this little liaison with good people or felt so deeply about those bloody Yanks. I hope they kept those scorecards and that they're all still trying to hit the wee white ba' somewhere on the planet.

If Harry and I had, somehow, given these marvellous people a few memories to take back over the pond with them, then there would have been no bigger success story to be told. I know now—through writing this bloody book—that those golfers and others like them have instilled into my soul some very special memories which will live with me for the rest of my days. Thanks, guys. God bless them all—whoever God might be.

Don't stop me now. I'm having a good time. I'm having a ball . . . Right on, Freddie!

Every One a Star!

A particularly satisfying time of the year was spring going into early summer. The course would be fairly easy to maintain as the growth would have barely begun, and the sight of the new lambs scampering all over the place was a pure joy to behold! I remember coming up the 5th hole with a customer, Howard Maylard, who was having a good game and had adapted to the hickory play very well.

As he teed up his ball and addressed it for the big hit with the brassie, half a dozen wee lambs pranced about, roughly eighty yards away, right in the middle of the fairway (what fairway?). They were playing on the overgrown ruins of a tiny chapel once situated exposed to the elements on the lower hillside and now on the fifth hole. The chapel would indeed have been very cold and totally exposed to every cauld blast during winter, hence, giving Coldchapel farm and its lands its name.

Howard swung his brassie with great intent and only succeeded in catching the ball halfway, resulting in a screaming daisy cutter about one foot of the ground. The ball whizzed off the clubface straight in line with the poor wee innocent lambs, and sure as shit, it hit one on the hind leg. Fuckin' ouch!

We heard the crack from the tee, and that wee lamb grew into a big ugly sheep with a fucked-up leg for the entirety of its life and limped its way into the abattoir later in the year. Howard was quite upset, and I had to reassure him that the lamb was actually OK. Liar! My heart went out to the wee thing every time I saw it on the course thereafter until it finally disappeared from the scene altogether. Lamb chops!

Sheep—I must have seen around three million of them in my first job at a local abattoir spanning a period of nine years before, regrettably, it went into receivership. It was the best job I ever had and the best bosses, the Jacksons, one could expect to have too! I can't remember any of the slaughter men needing counselling here!

Pleasingly and somewhat reassuring, the Red Letter Days' customers started phoning me up for their tee bookings and the info pack I would send out to all of them. One thing was for sure regarding all of the people who would make a visit to this wee golfing ground, they would all get the very best of attention and the very best service that I could possibly provide.

I would send them all a wee package giving accommodation details, directions to the course, other attractions in the area, local golf courses, and any other information on request. One of the first pairings I had was Daniel Symonds and his pal Phillip Edwards from the Midlands in England. Little did any of the customers ever know that before their arrival at Arbory I would have already done the nine hole circuit in preparation of their arrival. It was absolutely necessary that I go round all the greens and clear up any sheep shit on the greens, deposited from the previous day.

What a start to any day! I had to get up to the course, twelve miles from my home in Biggar, no later than seven o'clock in the morning. Once there, I would get my disposable gloves on, pick up my bucket, and get cracking! Normally, I could get round in just over an hour and have all the greens and a two-metre fringe clean and tidy. In the early days, a golf club would employ a couple of school children for this chore before the start of their Saturday medal competition. The job would be exactly the same as mine, but whether the kids had the benefit of protective gloves I wouldn't know.

Seeing the sanctuary of the pavilion was always a great relief, and there was comfort in the knowledge, provided that I had time, that a wee cuppa was waiting for me after a thorough wash and quick change of attire. The meenister always greeted the Red Letter Days' customers as that was primarily a part of the package.

Sometimes I would deliberately wait for people as they walked from the car park, hiding at the corner of the pavilion, then startle them as they ambled towards me. That got a good laugh before they'd even started the experience. The meenister was a big scary-looking bugger, even scaring me at times.

Daniel and Phil received their morning coffee and lecture from the meenister complete with his forthright views on the modern golfer and their equipment. The clubs and balls they were about to use were fully explained, while trying to reassure any nervous players that they should just relax and enjoy the day.

We had two types of ball for play: the gutta and the gutty. It was up to the player which ball they used, but I always stressed that they should first try the more user-friendly gutty and get acquainted with the clubs before even thinking about trying the very difficult gutta-percha!

They were about to embark on an old, but for them a new, experience, just like children learnt to play the game a hundred years ago! The experience was, pure and simply, a game of golf. Then it was out on to the course for the main proceedings of the day—hickory golf! As much as they wanted I would tell them, so long as they finished before dark, because that was when the course was reserved for our local ghostly spirits—free of charge, un-naturally.

On the first tee, I would demonstrate how to make a sand tee, by teeing up the first player's ball, just as an old caddie of yesteryear would have been expected to do. There was a sand box at every tee or wooden tee pegs in their bag if they preferred to use them. Last piece of advice before lift-off was the line of the hole and 'Swing slow—you're not going to hit the ball on the backswing!'

After this point, for me, it was a case of keeping my fingers crossed for each and every player. I'd already discovered from the few golfers that had already played with hickory that it wasn't just the high handicapper that would struggle badly with this particular game. Some guys who were playing off a single figure had suffered and failed to get to grips with the experience, proving just how forgiving the modern clubs really are.

Daniel, I found out later, had bought Phil the day out as a birthday gift. I think Daniel led the way with what was a good solid shot, and Phil started to take some practice swings. You can tell instantly with a golfer's grip and posture how they're about to fair before they even hit the ball. Phil was looking rather impressive in grip, stance, posture, and tempo of his swing. He most definitely . . . looked the part . . . and if you look the part at golf, you probably played the part too! This might not be too bad a start, I thought.

Sure enough, Phil got one well up the fairway (what fairway?) and just a short pitch from the green. We were off to a flyer, and I felt relaxed myself and began my blabbering about golf history. 'Now just ask anything you like, guys, and if I know I'll tell you. And if I don't know, I'll tell you I don't have a bloody Scooby. And if you've heard enough from me, just tell me to shut up, and I will!'

All sorts of stuff came up during a round, mostly depending on each customer's feedback. One standard ditty at the start of play was the old saying golfers had in the 1890s: '*Play the ball as it lies, and take the course as you find it!*' This couldn't be truer for Arbory, although I would stress the fact that there was no shame in any golfer taking a 'preferred lie' through the green.

The prime objective here was for the golfer to strike some good shots, even if it meant making life that little bit easier for them. Daniel played his second up and over the tiny first green while I stood next to Phil as he pondered his second shot, a short twenty-yard pitch. I noticed the ball was lying quite poorly and restated the option of taking a preferred lie.

'Ehm. I'll just play ball as it is, Alfie, if you don't mind,' he replied.

'Not at all, Phil. But if I can just warn you about the loft on the niblick. It's quite easy to go right under the ball with those niblicks, especially on a fluffy lie. Sometimes it's easier to try a wee bump and run with the mashie niblick when you're close enough to the green. It's how you see it and you'll learn as you go,' I uttered with instructive genius.

He then proceeded to gently flick the ball towards the flag and lay about eight feet from it. Daniel played out for a five, and Phil needed the two putts for his standard 'bogey' four. The *bogey* score was what a competent player would expect to play each hole in and was adopted for golf purposes in 1891 at Great Yarmouth.

Standing on the second tee, I explained the safe line and the more risky (out of bounds) 'best' line to play this one. 'This is where things get a bit more difficult on the next two holes. It's also where you should be enjoying the scenery and taking time to enjoy that too! The great Walter Hagen said, *"In life, never hurry, never worry, and don't forget to smell the flowers along the way."* You've got all day, and if you feel like dropping another ball at any time, just do it,' I told them.

The flamboyant Hagen also said about himself, *'I never wanted to be a millionaire. I just wanted to live like one!'* And he certainly did just that! Phil teed up and cracked one straight down the right-hand side, flirting with the out of bounds but finding the only flat piece of ground on this hole, just as the doctor had ordered.

Now, either Phil had got off to a good but fortunate start or he was actually a fairly competent player. We would soon find out when he played the long approach to the second green. I stuck with Phil going along the second and left Daniel to his own devices down below us on the lower lying ground. 'Right, Phil. I couldn't have placed that ball in a better position, and I see you've been rewarded with a reasonable lie as well. Now you can see the difference of being up here as opposed to Daniel down there.' I pointed towards Daniel. 'You'll probably need the midiron to reach the green, but being short isn't a bad result as the ground falls away rapidly at the back of the green,' I instructed once more, almost like a tour caddie.

Well, I should have known what to expect. He clipped the ball off the top of the ground as clean as a whistle, and it soared high and handsome from our elevated position towards the green down below, landing just a couple of yards short of the putting surface.

I was now truly impressed because those midirons, roughly the equivalent of a modern three, I found to be extremely difficult to hit clean! With a wee pat on the back, a few complimentary words, and a customary smile, I retrieved the club and put it back in the bag, and we made our way down towards the green where Daniel was waiting.

I would often act as caddie for a customer, giving them a free walk round the course and sharing my services if there was two or more.

It wasn't a heavy task as the bag was very light in comparison to the cumbersome burden the modern golfer hauls round the course today!

'Well, Daniel, how are you doing? I'm afraid I've been neglecting you thus far,' I said rather apologetically.'

'Oh, never mind me, Alfie. This is Phil's day. And I'm more than happy for you to give him your time,' he replied.

'That's very kind of you, Daniel. But I don't think this man needs much help from the likes of me!' I stressed with a laugh and left them both to putt out. It was usually on the second green that I would explain some of the pros and cons of the stymie and do my exhibition stuff again. How gratifying it was when I actually holed out by chipping over the opponent's ball, even more so when the customer managed this minor feat from golf's past themselves!

We were now on the third tee, and I started to state the options for this tricky bogey 4. 'You can either lay up in the middle ground there with an easy mashie (5 iron), leaving the longer approach, or if you're feeling brave, you should clear the ditch in the distance with a good drive with the brassie. But it will have to be a good one!' I stressed clearly.

While Phil withdrew the brassie from the bag without a moment's thought or hesitation, I wondered if I should satisfy my curiosity regarding Phil's occupation. I'd let him hit first.

He went through his routine and struck another fine drive. 'Och. This is too easy for you, Phil. That'll clear the ditch and some to spare,' I said while the ball was still in mid-flight. And so it did, landing well over the ditch and in prime position for a short approach to the green. 'Eh. What is it that you do for a living, Phil?' Daniel and Phil looked at each other with a semblance of guilt on their faces.

'Oh, perhaps I should have told you earlier, Alfie,' Phil said rather hesitantly.

'Tell me what, I'm intrigued,' I asked.

'I'm actually the professional at Coxmoor Golf Club, Alfie!' There was a short pause as we looked at each other in triplicate with heads nodding back and forth before we gave into simultaneous outburst of laughter.

'A bloody professional! Ya bugger! And here's me trying to give you tips. Ah bloody well knew it on the first tee, Phil!' I protested in fun while giving him a wee poke in the belly with my mashie niblick walking stick. This changed the perspective of the day for me, as I could now exploit Phil's obvious talent to the max, by asking *him* all sorts of questions!

Feedback was vital from the good, the bad, and with total respect . . . the downright ugly. This brings to mind Jack Lemmon who played every year in the Bing Crosby Pro-Am, but in 1993, his game was even worse than usual, and by the time Lemmon reached the 18th green he was so over par his partners had long since stopped counting—not, however, his caddie.

'I was lying 10 on the green and was left with a 35 foot putt,' recalled Lemmon. 'So I whispered over my shoulder and asked, 'How does this one break?' To which the caddie replied, 'Who fucking cares!'

We played on through the first nine holes, after which I would break off for the pavilion and put the kettle on for a cuppa. Then I would sit and bring before them the prized collection of balls we'd found on the course and a few other exhibits.

Everything was explained in detail—how the ball evolved and the effects on golf through each stage. Simmering away in the kitchen, I would have some ball-sized chunks of gutta softening up in an old pot. I loved some of the expressions on their faces when the customers saw me bringing forth to them this old dingy steaming pot and them wondering secretly, *'What the bloody hell is this?'*

'Now we don't want you to burn your fingers here, but you're now going to roll your very own gutta ball!' I exclaimed excitedly while sitting a chunk on the table in front of them. A wee demonstration followed, and then the pupils tried hand-rolling a ball for themselves. They were like primary kids in the classroom when they got some Plasticine to play with!

I also had Neil's prototype home-made feathery, with the feathers trying to squeeze out from its leather casing. It absolutely looked the part for describing to people—how they were made and what they looked like when they inevitably burst open.

'Right, gents. If you're ready, I think we should get back out there when the weather is with us. And when we finish, your lunch should be waiting for you both over at Toby's in the village.' And we headed for the first tee once more. 'The great thing about a nine hole course is that you should know where you're going on the second loop,' I declared.

They both had a couple of practice swings, and then Phil reached into the ball pocket and took out his gutta ball. 'I think I'll have a go with this one, Alfie, if that's OK with you?'

'Aha. You're the professional, Phil,' I said with emphasis. 'I wouldn't have expected any less from you. Good luck!' I told Phil that he would find it beneficial to play the ball more forward off the left foot and employ a slightly open stance at approach, in order to help get the ball airborne.

Away we went with Phil making good contact with his first shot with the gutta, but he showed surprise at how far it had travelled or rather how far it hadn't travelled! Almost immediately, both Phil and Daniel had learnt the lesson of scale between the types of ball you used against the course. He was obviously relishing this new challenge ahead.

My strategy was to take them up the first and along the second, where I would diplomatically divorce myself from the proceedings and walk back down to the pavilion. It meant that I could get a few phone calls in—check with Toby that the lunches were in order and any other minor tasks I may have to fulfil. It also served to give the customers an hour or so of respite from yours truly before I walked out to reunite with them—usually as they came over the hill at the seventh and into view from the pavilion.

I walked out when I saw them strolling along the seventh fairway (what fairway?) and escorted them to the green. Holes eight and nine ran parallel to each other with the eighth heading into the middle of the course. Phil was apparently doing quite well with the gutta ball, but I didn't ask to see his scorecard at this point.

We played up the eighth after the usual local knowledge was shared, and halfway through, I told them that I would be staying where I was so that I could give them the line to come back down the ninth. 'Just hit it straight over my head,' I told them, 'and preferably not through it!' They putted out and climbed up to the small tee cut into the hillside, and I gave them a wave to gain their attention.

Phil drove his gutta right over my head and on to the flattish plateau twenty yards beyond me and into position A for the approach. Daniel took the safer route, which left him a good bit further back. Arbory's greatest defence was the network of ditches weaving all over her twenty-five acres.

Phil assessed his second, a straightforward mashie niblick from a good lie, playing down on to the green from the elevated plateau—a nice wee shot to finish the round. He struck it well as was the norm for his status, and the ball climbed high and started to plummet towards the area of the green. 'Ach! I think you've pushed that one ever so slightly, Phil,' I said with disappointment. Sure enough, the ball landed a meagre ten yards or so, right of the green.

You have to remember that missing a green on Arbory was no disgrace, even to a competent pro. The third green was the biggest in area, and if the pin was cut in the centre, the longest putt you could have was about fifteen feet! We got down to the greenside and found ourselves puzzled as to where Phil's ball had finished. There was a muckle great patch of rushes short of the green, but he had definitely cleared those. Strange! Then we found it, with just a small trace of white paint to be seen, peeping up at us, totally plugged in a soft wet patch of turf.

'Ho ho! What are ye going to do with that one, Phil?' I declared—almost triumphantly. Here we were on a golf course that just didn't know how to forgive! The clubs, the balls, and the terrain. Phil had played the perfect drive followed by a perfect approach only to find himself totally scuppered for his third shot. The only problem is that on this tiny golf course on this tiny planet you don't get perfection! Phil looked at the ball, at least, what he could actually see of the ball, and then looked towards the flag only thirty-five feet away.

'You can take your preferred lie, Phil . . . if you really want to . . . ha ha,' I said sarcastically and probably quite annoyingly, as far as Phil was concerned. He looked at me with a glare. I was making fun of this situation, but Phil was taking a more professional approach.

He'd been given a good kick up the arse by Mother Nature, and he was trying to work out a way . . . to kick her right back! 'Hmmm! I'd like to play it as it lies, Alfie, if that's OK?'

'Fine by me, Phil. You're the professional,' I replied.

He wasn't too sure about something. 'What's the problem?' I asked.

'I'm worried I might break the club, Alfie.'

'Oh, bugger the club. I want to see this. Go for it, Phil, and don't you dare hold back!' I demanded. I knew what he had to do and could have offered him a spade which would have made the job so much easier.

He took up his stance and focussed his eye on the flag. Then his eye went back to the ball again and away we went—a slow controlled three-quarter backswing and whoosh! This was a mud shot, and when the clubhead pierced the ground, there was a spatter of muck flying in every direction—much like your standard sand blast, but not so pretty in the after-shock spray.

The three of us were keenly scanning the patch of air between Phil and the hole for some indication of a sphere. I could see a black blob trying to navigate its way towards the green, and lo and behold . . . that was the ball! It made it to the surface of the green and bobbled a couple of feet and lay only five feet from the stick.

I congratulated him on such a well-executed and improvised shot and told him bluntly, 'You'd better sink that bloody putt now or you're not getting any lunch!' Of course, he did sink that putt, and he revealed to me a score of 37, playing the ball as it lay with a gutta-percha! Bloody marvellous! It also turned out that Phil was very friendly with one of our pals, Stuart Callan, the pro at Bathgate, from whom Harry and I had received a long overdue series of golf lessons a few years back.

I escorted Phil and Daniel over to Toby's for their lunch, and they returned to the course an hour later to say cheerio and enter a comment in the visitors' book. Phil wrote in capital letters: 'THANK GOD FOR TECHNOLOGY!' The day for me was a learning curve and a very pleasing and enjoyable one at that.

I was ecstatic in myself that I had performed well that day and that this format of entertaining the customers would be my benchmark for those who would follow. Even so, I was knackered, and there was no time for sitting on my laurels because those damned sheep were shitting all over the place. Somebody would have to try and keep up with them. I didn't have to wonder who.

On another occasion, I was taking a fourball round and had reached the short 4th hole, where I usually gave a small demonstration with my mashie niblick which I used mostly as a walking stick. It wasn't something that I liked doing, but I felt compelled to put my own humility on the spot, especially for those who might be struggling with their game.

The 4th was a great wee hole of only 100 yards from an elevated tee with a small pond to clear and a ditch guarding the front of the green. The green itself being rather tiny fell away to the rear where the long ball would find its way rolling down the hill and into another ditch!

This little show had evolved from some of the first customers who had actually demanded that I show them how it was done. Of course, sometimes it wasn't a very pretty display of my golfing skills. But on this occasion, I teed up the ball, chattering all the time as Trevino would, quoting this or that and emphasising the need for a slow controlled swing and stating my biggest tip—that nobody ever hits the ball on the backswing!

Easy did it—and then through the ball with a wee punch. Sweet as a nut, the ball flew effortlessly off the clubface to its highest elevation before beginning to drop softy. Hmmm. That looks quite good for line, I was thinking, as it just seemed to hang in the air forever.

Down it came with the admiring gallery watching intently and sat in its own pitchmark four inches left and pin high of the hole. 'How will that do?' I exclaimed in self-contained delight and maybe a slight element of shock. And a round of applause was accorded to me and the shot.

One of the guys retorted immediately, 'Dae that again and ah'll gie ye a tenner.' To which I accepted the challenge with an approving nod and proceeded to hit another fine shot. This time though I put just a little bit of cut spin on the ball or maybe it was just a wee puff of wind, but it feathered ever so slightly to the right, but still only six feet from the stick.

I did have the bugger worried for his tenner! Oh, how I wish I'd cut that hole four inches to the left and perhaps given myself my second ace and, as far as we know, the first recorded hole in hole at Abington. Damn! Jeest a wee tap in birdie two though.

Another one of my party tricks was to act as caddie and re-enact the role of the old caddie who'd had enough of his learned master on the links one day, but who was neither learned nor master to golf! The young cleric had been duffing and foozling and sclaffing his way round the course till the old caddie ran out of patience. He threw the clerics clubs to the ground in disgust and declared, *'Their's yer sticks—dinnae disgrace a professional!'* And he walked off in a tantrum.

This experience was all about getting people to relax and be cheerful while tackling the hardest sport of them all. My caddie tantrum never failed to get some hearty laughs. Fun and laughter, that's what golf should be about.

I'll never forget the day I was up on the course digging land drains with my pick and shovel. Underneath the mossy sward of turf lay nothing but stones, which made for heavy going with hand-held implements! There were patches on the course, where it was quite different and where the ground was very soft and peaty, but not today!

The month of May had been another cold, wet, and miserable affair, and I'd just about had enough given that my hands were aching, thanks to the pick ricocheting off stone after stone. I was like one of those cartoon characters being vibrated by every other stroke of the pick—dongggg. 'Fuck this, I'm going down for a cuppa and a heat up.'

So I waddled my way down the hill to the Portakabin, where my flask was waiting for me. With a big sigh come grunt, I kicked some of the muck off my wellies, entered the kabin, and plonked myself down on my plastic chair. 'Ah. That's better.' I had just managed to pour a cuppa from the flask and taken the first refreshingly warm sip when the phone rang. 'Och. Who the fucks this?' I wondered with defeated pessimism.

A deep, rustic voice enquired, 'Is thish Alfie Ward I'm shpeaking to?'

This voice sounded somewhat familiar.

'Yes—speaking,' I answered.

'Sean Connery here.' . . . A short pause had me thinking, Is this some smart bastard taking the piss at such a time that it just wouldn't be appreciated? It wasn't! Months earlier, we had sent Sean a down-to-earth (but highly complimentary) letter accompanied by a dozen of the very best painted guttas we had left in our rapidly diminishing stock. A bloody good present for any golfer whether adorned with a knighthood or not!

'I'm in Prague filming at the moment and thought I'd give you a call,' he said.

'That's really kind of you. I appreciate that,' I replied gratefully and somewhat bemused.

'Absholutely! I'm coming home to Scotland on Wednesday week to take in the European Cup Final . . . ,' he continued.

The pessimistic gremlins had been banished in a nanosecond, replaced by rejuvenated optimism of the highest order! This could be the biggest break imaginable—Scotland's number two son (Wallace being number one) coming to Arbory. Hey, life wasn't so bad after all. By this time I was sitting upright, the damp and cold no longer a factor. My brain was turning into mince with all the different messages being sent to and fro from various parts of that six-inch space between the ears—the most important part of any golfer's persona. When was he coming . . . for how long? . . . What would he need for food? . . . Do we keep this low profile and private? . . . But I do need to exploit this—shurely! Then . . .

'But I'm afraid I won't have time to make a visit to your golf course.'

'Ah fuck!' Via soliloquy, of course.

He then continued to explain how his producers just wouldn't give him time off and everything on this latest film was being run on a tight time schedule. The conversation died a horrible death from my perspective, and tones were passing overhead and from one ear and straight out the other.

Here I was, in a shithole of a Portakabin on a typically pissing wet day, talking to one of the most famous and popular actors of all time and he was Scottish, a nationalist like myself, an ardent golfer, almost sharing the same birthday! That moment had almost arrived—I just didn't know whether to laugh or cry.

Trying to remain upbeat, I began to wind the call up, 'Well, I hope you enjoy the final, Mr Connery. And thanks again for taking the time to call me.'

'Absholutely. I wish you well with your golf business, Alfie,' he said sincerely.

And that was that, with a goodbye from him and a cheerio from me.

I got up from my chair and had a look around this howf I was in. The dampness from my leggings had soaked through to my arse, and I tried to pick the sticking underpants away from my cold flesh while taking up the bandy leg posture, as you do. I looked outside to see the empty pavilion being drenched in the continuing rainfall.

I lit my fag and inhaled a good puff just to ease the tension and gave a wry smile to myself, huh—then kicked a nearby chair with the soul of my boot to send it skidding along the floor to the end of the Portakabin where it could easily have gone straight through the decaying wall! Temper—temper.

Thankfully, no damage was sustained to the chair or the kabin, and my foot escaped injury too.

Ach well, I feel better now. But where's Harry? *He* would have some ideas on this. Might as well finish my cuppa and have a cheese peece, I thought.

I began asking myself questions, mostly because there was no one else there to bounce them off. Who can I tell about this? Who would believe me? What's the point anyway? Maybe I should give young Craig at the *Gazette* a call to see what he thinks of it all? Aye! That's exactly what I'll do.

And so it was. I gave Craig a call and started to explain the euphoria of my ten-minute conversation with *the* original and best James Bond esquire.

'Hi, Craig, it's Alfie here. Thought I'd give you a wee call with the latest.'

'What's happening, Alfie?' he replied.

'Oh, I've just had Sean Connery on the phone. He's coming back to Scotland next week,' said I, with a hint of knowledgeable arrogance.

'What! You're kidding me, right?'

'Not at all, Craig. But don't get too excited. He's not coming up to the course.' And I then fully explained the conversation in detail.

Craig appeared to be getting all excited about this breaking news, but I was confounded as to why. 'Listen to me, Craig. He's not coming to Arbory,' I tried to stress upon his apparently deaf ears.

'Of course, he is, Alfie. Leave it with me. I should be able to get this out in this week's paper!' Craig exclaimed while hurriedly saying his goodbyes and hanging up the phone on me.

What exactly Craig was up to I just didn't know, but he obviously had something in mind which would make for an interesting few days later on, after he had published his story. He was streetwise and I wasn't. Harry would have known what he was up to. For now, I would have my tea and cheese peece, but there was still work impending on the course. I couldn't relax simply because 'Big Tam' had been on the blower.

A couple of days elapsed before Craig came back to confirm that he was ready to run with the Connery story and whether it was OK to proceed. 'Aye, charge on with whatever you've got, Craig. What harm can it do?' And so it was. *The Gazette* came out on the Thursday, and by Friday morning, my mobile was red hot and nearing meltdown!

I kid you not. I had every UK national newspaper on my case wanting to know when they should be at the course with *their* reporter. I just didn't have the savvy or gumption to play them along and stupidly lost my opportunity by playing it straight. I told every one of them that he unfortunately had to cancel due to his other commitments, but said that they could still send a reporter and get a story from it. None of them took me up on my begging offer. It was a case of give me Sir Sean Connery or go lose yourself! Another case of so near and yet so far.

One of the funnier moments came when I was sitting in the kabin having a cuppa after I'd made a batch of gutta balls. I'd left the door open to let the steam from the boiling gutta pot and my fag smoke escape. The kabin wasn't used for the customers any more, since we had a shiny bright pavilion for them. To be honest, the place had gotten a bit dingy, and Harry the spider had been busy weaving his webs at the corners of the windows. Those webs weren't doing any harm, and I usually left them alone rather than callously destroy the spider's work of art, just for the sake of it!

Buzzzzzz! A muckle great bumble bee decided to come in for a look and rumbled all over place, bumping into the glass of the windows, as they do. The bee found its way to the window I was sitting at and started, annoyingly, buzzing up and down the glass, bumping and rumbling. Then it dropped right down and rumbled into the spider's web.

Aw, what a pity, I thought (for the spider). The bee was entangled, and the vibrations of the web obviously alerted Harry of a potential customer and he promptly came out of hiding. He was a big black bugger but clearly not big enough, because he instantly fled back into the window frame. I imagined the spider saying, 'Oh bugger! You're far too big for me to handle, and you've wrecked my bloody web!' The bee managed to free itself and flew out the door. The incident made me laugh aloud and momentarily eased the stress.

Then there was the English couple who called in on their way home after a golfing trip to St Andrews. I can't remember their names, so we'll call them the Smiths. I think they had been tipped off about Abington by the good people at The Dunvegan Hotel in St Andrews.

It was just luck that I happened to be at the course when they arrived. I introduced myself and invited them into the pavilion where I put the kettle on. 'Can I make you a cuppa?' I asked.

'Oh yes. That would be lovely thank you. It's been a couple of hours since we left St Andrews,' Mrs Smith replied.

I talked up the golfing marvels of the '*auld grey toon*' as the kettle boiled, then enquired if they intended to play here at Abington. 'Yes, if that's possible, Alfie,' she said with a smile. 'Not a problem in the slightest, Mrs Smith. But we do things a little differently here. I'll get your teas and give you a summary of the experience, then you can make up your mind if you still want to play.'

I told them the fee for the golf and club hire and gave them their tea and a plate of biscuits, and then I went into one! I explained the hickory concept, while showing them the clubs and the balls in use. After about twenty minutes of nattering, I asked them what they wanted to do. Mr Smith stated that he was the golfer and that his wife would just be walking the course with him. But both agreed that 'this place' was absolutely fascinating.

To cut a long story short, I gave them the full treatment on the course, and when we'd finished, another cuppa was brewed up and enjoyed by all three of us. When we had finished our tea, I offered them another nine holes free of charge, which was politely declined. 'I'd love to, but we've got a long drive in front of us to get home, Alfie. So we'd better head off soon,' Mr Smith declared.

'How much do we owe you for this splendid day out?' Mrs Smith asked.

'Oh, just what we agreed at the start, Mrs Smith. I think I said £25, didn't I?'

She was quite surprised and taken aback. 'Yes, you did. But surely that's not enough? What about the teas we've had and your time?' she asked.

'Och. That's just part of the package. What's a couple of tea bags and some hot water amongst friends, eh? I'm not here to rip folk off. That won't save this place, will it? I'll leave that to the rest of Scotland's tourism industry! Anyway, it was a wee bonus for me to catch you here today. I'm missing people all the time, so I'm just glad that you've been able to experience this.' They both shook their heads and thanked me for the hospitality.

They gathered their few bits and bobs, and Mr Smith made for the door while Mrs Smith shook my hand and thanked me again at the same time sticking a twenty in my hand. 'Oh no, no, no! There's no need for that. You've paid your dues,' I exclaimed.

'Please take it, Alfie.' . . . I interrupted, refusing the money again and stating that I should be thanking them for coming in. 'Listen to me,' she said. 'You don't understand. We've had a wonderful end to our holiday in Scotland.' . . .

Interrupting again, I argued, 'But . . .'

She pulled my arm and gave a stern look that clearly said, 'Just shut your bloody face, son.' So I did.

'No. Please listen to me. Jim had always wanted to go on his pilgrimage to St Andrews, but we'd never got round to it. The place *is* marvellous up there, but we came away very disappointed by the cost of everything. On the way down here, we both agreed that the box was now ticked and that . . . we would never be back in Scotland!' She smiled and looked into my eyes. 'But you've changed all that, Alfie. This place is like a breath of fresh air, and you've made us think again. This was better than St Andrews! Maybe we'll be back with some friends some day. Keep up the good work and stick with it. Thank you so much.'

I still choke when I think of that parting, as I do with so many others. If only I could have convinced the powers of enterprise that 'this place' was indeed special. Then . . . who knows?

And as far as St Andrews is concerned, it is undoubtedly an incredibly special place regardless of the tourism exploitation going on there. However, I also believe that every golf course on the planet is an incredibly special place! Bad golf course? Never seen one in my life!

Unearthing the Soul of Golf

Going into June 2002 and the frustrations continued on and off the course. People were turning up at the course in dribs and drabs, and the feedback was fantastic, enough to enlighten a heavy heart and raise hopes, albeit in brief spurts, before the lows set back in.

I was working intermittent shifts with Ronnie and getting up to the course at nights to do as much as I could, but it was a losing battle! I was getting sick of locals informing me that I had missed people at the course when I hadn't been there. Bad enough for me, but simply unacceptable for my customers.

But what else could I do? Jimmy from the caravan park gave me a poem to help me make up my mind as to what I should or shouldn't do:

> Success is failure turned inside out—
> The silver taint of the clouds of doubt—
> And you never can tell how close you are,
> It may be near when it seems afar;
> So stick to the fight when you're hardest hit—
> It's when things seem worst that you mustn't quit!

I've never been a quitter, or at least I don't think I have. Golf isn't a game of quitters, and perhaps that's one of the reasons I've been so obsessively fascinated with the sport all my life. Maybe this wasn't a case of quitting, but more in line with being sensible and thinking of the rest of my family.

Life is a one shot game, and to me, this business was my one shot at trying to make an impact in the world. Many charities would benefit in future years from this apparently innocuous business as they had done, albeit moderately, in the last two years. Was this so selfish an ambition to have? I still foresaw a good living to be had from hickory golf and a few jobs for others, including Harry if I could entice him back—if only I could turn it around.

And what of Scottish golf tourism? These Red Letter Days' customers were coming from all over Britain, and they were coming specifically to Abington for hickory golf. Some were using the visit as their excuse for making that holiday to Scotland they'd always meant to have, but hadn't got round to it. They would spend their welcome cash in hotels, B&B's, restaurants, shops, or whatever, and it was all thanks to hickory golf!

I worked out a very conservative estimate of the probable spend of *my* 100 RLD customers at around £50,000 for 2002. What if, and it was highly possible, that RLD sold three, four, or five times that many for next year? It didn't matter what I told those funders—they just couldn't see the value of this attraction. I was told by one as we sat looking out of the big pavilion window to the course, 'I don't have your vision.'

Even more annoying was the fact that an octogenarian millionaire lurked in the background, who just didn't have a fuckin' clue about doing the right thing. My late and lamented mother would quote the true and morbid adage of 'those' people and their money: '*A shroud disnae huv pockets, Son. They cannae tak it wae them!*'

To be fair, she was helping out with some cash here and there, but it amounted to token crumbs, where I really needed a wholesome loaf of bread! I was way past the point of wanting any of her money by now, anyway. Unfortunately, the potential funders also knew she was in the background, and one told me, unofficially, that she wasn't doing my case any good by being there. Great!

To hell with everybody else. I didn't think I'd been selfish at any or perhaps many times in my life to date, so . . . bugger it, I'm going to be a wee bit selfish now, at least until such times that I know that I'm totally fucked or I drop dead and get kicked off the ground.

On the bright side, there were a couple of positives also lurking in the background. I had a visit from Paul Lawrie to look forward to, and that golf writer from the States could do a good write-up for me. Lots of good advertising were coming up, and all of it was essentially free . . . as it had to be.

The *Telegraph* reporter John Gibb emailed to say that they were now looking at setting up Nick Faldo instead of Paul Lawrie for a 'hickory' session sometime at the end of June, provided John's editor approved of the gig. I put a sign up at the pavilion giving my apologies to anyone I was missing at the course and my mobile number if they wanted to contact me. Sure, this was pish, but what else could I do? Just have to persevere and keep talking to that Big Guy in the sky!

The system continued with me working a day or two, then returning to the course the next day to honour a booking, then away working again, and the shit kept on falling and waiting for my return. John Gibb confirmed that Faldo was a goer and we just had to tie down a time and date for the visit. That was fixed for 29 June at 5.30 p.m. in the evening.

Various pro golfers were raising concerns about how far the ball was being allowed to be developed by the manufacturers and the distances being attained. Although there were conformity guidelines set in place by the ruling bodies, the manufacturers were outsmarting and threatening litigation against the rule makers if they tried to stop them from making those golf balls!

The smart golfers, including our Nick, Crenshaw, Nicklaus, Woosnam, Lyle, Norman, Ward, and many others, realised that this just wasn't good for the sport in general, and a few golf writers brought the issue to the fore in their columns.

The world has never been in short supply of abundance of pure greed! Most of us are guilty of this frailty of mankind in some form or another, and golfers are no exception to the rule. Since the inception of the Haskell golf ball at the start of the twentieth century, golfers have found themselves embroiled in a senseless and futile greed for distance campaign!

The best analogy I can think of is the obsession of man with the length of his penis. The Haskell was the spark that ignited a hugely detrimental effect on the entire sport for the following century, turning its God-given architecture upside down! And so it continues to this day.

Why we didn't learn from the effects of the Haskell may have more to do with the mass commercialism of the sport and the beginnings of the manufacturer pandering to the whims of the consumer. Why the ruling bodies, on both sides of the pond, failed pathetically over the term of a century to protect the sport from 'the ball must go long' syndrome is another question!

Nick was planning to play a game at Muirfield during the day and head for Abington later. He would play nine holes with hickory and gutta, and John would write up his experience which would ultimately argue that the ball does not have to go long in golf.

This was going to be a whole load of fun, but I'd decided to keep the whole thing low-key until a few days before the event. I would invite my few members and the kids from the village and perhaps a few others. I didn't want this opportunity to turn into a total fiasco with people meandering all over the place and upsetting our Nick.

A decision had already been made in regards to the state of the course for this particular visit. It would have to be clean and at its best, and I would probably need to dedicate an entire week of my time to get it that way, regardless of where I was working at the time. Once I'd seen Nick's visit out of the way, I would then consider the visit of the American golf writer, James Dodson.

So I plodded on with a maniacal regime of trying to be at the course as and when I could, sometimes going up to Abington in the evenings and using the summer light till eleven o'clock—pickin' that fuckin' shite most of the time!

One night as I was walking up the first hole towards the green, I heard a distress call. Bugger! It was an old blackface ewe stuck firmly in the boggy area that lay off the line of the course. She was up to her belly in muck and had no way of getting free. As I approached, I could see that she was getting distressed, and she made a desperate but futile attempt to get out.

As a rule, sheep are ugly buggers (but their wee lambs are cute) with horrible piercing albino-like eyes, and this one was no exception to the rule. I grabbed the horns on her head and tried to pull her out, but with little success. If I continued with this strategy, I was risking pulling her bloody head off altogether! I was going to have to walk back down to the tool shed and get a spade to ease the suction of the muck from around her body, which was gluing her to the spot.

When I got back up to her, she was still terrified of me and distressed, but I got to work immediately. It only took a couple of minutes of digging into the soft peat before she started to slacken off, and then I grabbed her horns again and gave a good bloody tug.

'There ye go, ya daft auld bugger,' I exclaimed while pulling her clear of the ditch. Aghh, Christ's sake! She'd obviously been there quite a while because the maggots had been busy feasting on her legs! They were red raw but would heal given time. Nature doesn't hang about. She's a hard bitch at times.

I cleaned the maggots off and left her to settle and hopefully get back to her feet as I went up to the green forty yards away. After about fifteen minutes, I headed back down to see how she was getting on. She wasn't! I had thought she would have recovered enough to scramble back up on to her feet, but she was still too weak.

I grabbed the fleece on her back and gave a good yank to pull her up, using my shins as an anchor. She was bloody heavy! I did manage to get her to a standing position, but there was no strength to keep her up. So I just let her lie down and pulled some clumps of grass and laid them next to her head.

Funny? Part of our stock control regime was to chase those buggers up the hill when the course was dirty, and there was simply too many of them grazing on the bottom slopes of the course. We would throw golf balls at them and even clubs to chase them away so they'd shit somewhere else. A good dug would have saved us a whole lot of effort and angst.

The sheep were an integral factor of the whole experience, but a bloody nightmare to clean up after when they'd been on the course too long. They had the whole of Arbory Hill to feast upon, but they just couldn't stay away from the lower slopes of the golf course.

There wasn't much more I could do, so I went off and got some work done before it got dark. Before I went home, I walked back up and tried to get her on to her feet once more, this time with just a little success because she managed to stand for a couple of minutes before dropping down again. This was encouraging because I was thinking that the circulation was perhaps returning to those legs. By now, it was dark, and I had to get home. I would check up on her the next day, but hopefully, she would have recovered enough to walk off on her own.

The next day I made my way up the hill to check out the auld Blackie. She was still there but had, somehow, managed to transport herself twenty yards away from the boggy ditch that had entrapped her. I approached again, but this time she hardly displayed any signs of concern at my presence.

She was still just as ugly as the night before. I grabbed a horn on her head and the fleece at her rump and pulled her up to a standing position. Any sheep lying on its back will soon perish, and often all it takes to save a healthy sheep is to roll it over so that it can get back up.

She stood there motionless, balancing against the support of my legs but making no effort to walk off, and those albino-type eyes appeared to evoke hopelessness. This was a lost cause, I began to think, alas, like the land we were both standing upon! I gave up, knowing that I had, at least, made the 'try' for her, just as I was making the 'try' for Arbory.

The following day, I returned to the same spot and found that auld Blackie lying motionless . . . deid! I had anticipated its demise because I consciously took a shovel with me to do the needful and bury her out of sight. A farming trait which is now illegal! At least she was spared the butcher's knife, and I buried the old lady back in the bog whence she first got herself stuck! All in a day's work for the golf course manager.

So much was going on at the same time, and there simply weren't enough hours in each day to keep abreast of things. The Red Letter Days' customers kept trickling in and going away happy with their day out, while the odd stragglers appeared out of the blue and I managed to get a few green fees from them. I would spend as much time sending out emails in the evenings till the early hours and getting the administrative stuff out of the way.

Neil continued to appear for a game now and again, and I was always pleased to see him drive into the car park with Molly, his faithful old Labrador. Sometimes I would play nine holes with him, and I could see that his game was definitely improving.

How ironic, I would think, that here was a guy who had never played golf before yet defiantly insisted on playing Arbory with his hickories only! Several times I had tried to persuade him into taking the easy option of trying some modern clubs, but every time the suggestion was rejected out of hand. I admired that tremendously and wondered why established golfers appeared to be scared stiff of trying the experience.

His feather golf balls were improving too, as compared to his first attempt that I now used as a valuable exhibit for my customers with its feathery guts spilling out of its casing! Neil had turned into a really good friend and even offered an injection of his personal savings to try and save the business! A very humbling offer that I just couldn't accept.

It was around this time that I was busy trying to get the course signage sorted out. The idea was to make an A0 sign for every tee position filled with local and national historical golfing facts. This was the solitary piece of public funding sourced from Scottish Enterprise that I was likely to get, but it was welcome just the same—not in the priority areas where I desperately needed some cash, but criteria didn't allow assistance in those critical areas.

Our friends at Pro Sports had churned out ten sign posters in total, which included a welcome sign for the roadside. Harry and I had erected the eight-foot posts to support the signs just before his departure from proceedings, so I just had to find some kind of support for the back of them and get them up. It would all add to the character of the place, and Ronnie came to the rescue by supplying the ply board, sealant, and trims that were necessary to get the job done. Once in place, I have to say that they were looking pretty damn good!

So much so that on one occasion the signs caused a serious case of slow play on the course! I had two Red Letter Days' customers, father and son, Clive and Gareth Bennett. I escorted them through the first nine holes complete with all the trimmings, and we retired to the pavilion for tea and further lecturing.

I was feeling quite exhausted and decided to let them go back out on their own, especially since Mrs Bennett was also walking the course with them. After about ninety minutes, I began to wonder where they had got to because they should have been back in sight of the pavilion by now. They were both good players, and Gareth had been a schoolboy champion down south.

So I headed over the hill and saw them in the distance at the 6th tee. They were busy taking photos and video footage at every single tee where the signs were located!

Of course, there wasn't a problem with this in the slightest; we didn't worry too much about slow play on this course, but I just had to kid them on about causing slow play, which got a few laughs.

When they did eventually return to home base, I performed my little demonstration on the evolution of the ball. Keeping things simple, I would use my modern 8 iron to play three shots towards the 6th green: one with a gutta, one with our replica gutty, and the last with a modern bullet. The results were obvious, with the bullet surpassing the previous two efforts by quite a distance!

My pièce de résistance was to have my own Big Bertha Callaway lurking in the background, which had the customers wondering why such a piece of scrap metal should ever grace such an historical place. Their curiosity was soon answered when I would tee up a bullet and take my stance. Then I would tie a scarf round my head for a blindfold and ask somebody to address the clubhead to the ball.

Of course, I was taking the piss out of the modern game and how it had been allowed to be simplified by the rule makers! Nice and easy, low and slow, and here's hoping the joke wouldn't backfire. I never missed that risqué shot whenever I was in the mood to try it. Easy-peasy this modern *game* of golf!

Occasionally, I would hear reports of different newspapers and magazines who would tout the cause in small articles. The *Sunday Mail* published one which highlighted the contact with Sir Sean and had a good go at the funding system in general! The *Scots Magazine* also published a nice feature, but nothing seemed to be drumming up anything like the business which I so urgently needed. The business needed a fast-talking whizz-kid of a salesman, but there was no way I could fund that, even though it was probably the sensible way to go. The days and weeks were passing, and before I knew it, we were heading for the end of June.

John Gibb informed me that the Nick Faldo visit was definitely arranged for the evening of Saturday 29 June, and therefore, I had a week to get everything in order. I knew I had a ball-bursting time in front of me, but there was a good chance this would be my last throw of the dice. All in all, when the course was free and clean of sheep shit, it looked really great and all that it should be. The added visual of the signs made it look like the attraction it was supposed to be.

But an event such as this was a real uplift to the morale, which made the task in hand so much easier than it actually was. I didn't have the pure luxury of hiring John Gibson's quad bike and sweeper machine, much as I would have loved to. I worked away all week dedicating every ounce of my energy and every second of my time in getting Arbory ready for a real high-profile visit.

Saturday came along and . . . hey! It was a beautiful summer's day and the golfing gods appeared to be on my side, for a change. That was until John phoned me about lunchtime. I was standing at the second green high up on the course and admiring my handiwork, wearing my best dudes and feeling rather pleased with myself.

Faldo's PA had just phoned him to say that he wouldn't be flying north due to an eye infection he'd picked up from his kids. John himself was phoning from Edinburgh airport where he was trying to get on to the next flight south to London. A wasted trip for him too! I walked over to the ninth tee thirty yards away where a bench seat was waiting. I sat down and had a fag and then began wondering what the hell was going on with this dream come nightmare?

All dressed up with nowhere to go—I was bent over with my head in hands, and for all I knew or cared, the fag I'd lit was possibly singeing my hair. Someone was having a laugh at my expense, and I looked up at the clear blue sky. I couldn't work out the logic of this self-inflicted examination of character, so another fag was ignited. Then another . . . and another.

I could hear the squeals of the buzzards and looked up into the blue sky once more, and there they were, soaring and riding the thermals high above Arbory. Oh well! It was only two o'clock in the afternoon, and I'd better let the few people I had invited to the golf show know that it was just another in a growing line of disappointments.

The only consolation of the whole affair was that Faldo withdrew from the European Open in Ireland the following week, and that meant that the call off was entirely genuine. Just my luck! And I'm almost certain that Nick would have relished this little challenge too. Who could say that one of Britain's finest golfers had gone and got bloody sick on them?

By mid-July, I was feeling as low as I'd ever been in my life. I hadn't felt this bad since Mum died, and embarrassingly, I found those feelings and emotions comparable to one another when they probably shouldn't be.

The dribs and drabs continued, and I thought, Now if only the Red Letter Days singles were fourballs, then I'd be cooking with gas, and then I could say that I had a real business to run. But they weren't fourballs, and the overdraft facility of £10,000 was nearing its limit. Armageddon was on the horizon, and even I could see that now!

I got a phone call from James Dodson, and he told me he was still committed to writing up an article for *Golf Magazine* (the biggest selling golf magazine in the States) on Arbory Braes. He emailed me a few days later, confirming that he would like to visit the course at the end of August and that his editor had given him a target of around 2,000 words for the feature. Obviously, this feature wasn't going to be tucked into an obscure column somewhere in the magazine.

I continued to make appeals to our fire-raising tourism minister, South Lanarkshire's Labour Council, and Scottish Enterprise with inevitable results. On the last day of July, the course had a true drainage test. It had been raining constantly, highlighted by two torrential thunderstorms. I'd never seen anything like it, and it came as no surprise to see the Raggengill burn at the rear of the pavilion come down in spate!

The road was flooded to the extent that it would not have been sensible to try and cross the flood in a car. The rain eased off at seven in the evening, and I decided to go up on to the course and evaluate any damage sustained by the deluge. I could hardly believe my eyes, because the entire course was perfectly playable with only a few areas holding water!

Talking of water, my brother Pat and his son Michael came all the way from Hawick to fix the hot water heater which had been out of action for quite a while. What a plush wee pavilion we had again. It was Pat, a sport parachutist in his younger days, who saw me through my one and only parachute jump during the 1970s—an incredible experience considering my lifelong affliction with vertigo! Right now, I would be happy to jump out of the same door-less Cessna Skywagon—without the parachute!

So much was happening before my eyes. You just had to open your eyes and look. Harry's ponds were evolving daily with unidentified vegetation beginning to take hold—probably some kind of pond weed? Beautiful luminescent dragon flies were skimming the surface of the water too. Mushrooms and fungi were prevalent all over the course, and one customer even reported back, quite excitedly, that he had spotted valuable chanterelles growing on the course.

Neil told me that wild orchids were growing in the rough grass halfway up the first fairway (what fairway?), but the bloody sheep had got there before I could get up to see them. I absolutely loved the wild violas that grew in abundance in the higher parts of the course, and I would jest with the customers, 'You'd better not stand on my wild violas or there will be trouble!' All the ditch areas had healed nicely, and the blue of the forget-me-nots flourished in all the ditches.

We had created an entirely new environment simply by tinkering with nature and trying to persuade her that this tiny patch of land was now under our jurisdiction—under new management. And we also knew that we would have to keep a close eye on it as it would be delicate and volatile and susceptible to the whims of those bloody golfers, if there were too many of them on the course. Hmmm. Aye sure!

By the time James Dodson arrived at the end of August, I had let the course lapse to the sorry state of shitty appearance. I had also taken some time to do a little research on this writer of whom I, in my deepest ignorance, knew very little of. But arrive he did with his friend Patrick. They were both good players with Jim playing off a handicap of four and

Patrick eleven. We sat in the pavilion and had a cuppa while Jim taped an interview with me, and I gave him a low-down on what 'this place' was all about and how things were going with it.

Unfortunately, that included an apology for the state of the course and the reasons why that should be. It wasn't a day for mincing my words, and Jim wasn't slow to pick up on that little factor. My sentiments towards the R&A would be mentioned in his future article.

On a really blustery day, we went out and played the course where I explained the clubs and balls and various bits and bobs of golfing history. Having equipped them with their clubs and balls, we headed up for the first tee, and I asked Jim, 'So why have you come to Scotland, Jim?'

He looked at me slightly puzzled and replied, 'Why? We've come here for you, Alfie!'

'Really! I exclaimed in bemusement, because I genuinely thought his main task would be to write up Turnberry or St Andrews or one of the big boys in Scottish golf.

'Absolutely. We've heard quite a lot about Arbory Braes in the States. So here we are.'

After nine holes, we came back in for another cuppa and to finish off the interview. They were moving on to Turnberry, I think, and time was getting on, so they prepared to leave. Completely against my protestations, Jim insisted on giving me a considerable bung which more than covered an actual green fee, which left me slightly embarrassed because here was someone trying to help me and who more than deserved a freebie!

As they prepared to leave, I said to Jim, 'So, Jim, you've seen it and you've played it. I want you to be completely honest with me, Jim. What do you really think of this place?'

He looked at me and thought for a moment . . . '*Well, Alfie, I think that you and your brother have unearthed the soul of golf!*' That comment, from such a distinguished golf writer, was enough to make me choke, and I struggled to conceal my emotions at that moment.

Strong handshakes were exchanged, and off they went on their travels. I was left thinking about Harry and how he would have lapped up this fun day with Jim and Patrick. I also knew that this morale-boosting visit which perched me up on one of those elevated highs would be short-lived before the depressing lows set in once more.

Another long winter was looming once more, but the people kept on trickling in, which gave me just enough incentive, and hope, to stick with it and get on with the arduous task of raking the moss out of the greens. It was a case of déjà vu, and my stomach muscles were in for their annual workout.

Ronnie kept me going with paid work here and there although I wasn't bringing in nearly enough, and all sorts of shit was hitting the fan at home! Jim Dodson sent me a copy of the article he wrote for *Golf Magazine*, which would be inserted in the January 2003 edition.

Neil kept on popping up now and again and was always a welcome excuse for me to take a break from the labours of the course and have a wee natter and perhaps play a few holes with him. One night, he produced the round and fully stitched up feathery ball which I knew he would make successfully some day. We played a few *careful* shots with it, being wary not to burst it wide open, and what great fun that was.

Around October, I had letters from John Cowan and his friend Bob Templeton from Ayrshire, trying to help me out with advice and support. John had played the course as a Red Letter Days' customer and obviously identified the potential and unique selling point of the experience. Although their time and effort was greatly appreciated, I think I had all but given up hope at this time. Great and considerate people!

Christmas had arrived and my conscience was playing havoc with my mind, given the financial mess I had managed to create. Phil Edwards and Mrs Hayes sent Xmas cards with messages of encouragement enclosed, which helped to ease those feelings of guilt. I couldn't be bothered with the hypocrisy of adult Christmas anyway. It is great for the kids, but I can't get my head round all those adults being good Christians—for a day.

Somebody needs to tell them that there're 365 of them every year! Bah humbug!

Guid Folk, Ne'er-do-wells, and Coos

Happy New Year!

I got a phone call from a young American couple, Brian Gracely and his fiancé, Amy, who were in Turnberry and wanted to come make a flying visit. Naturally, I confirmed a booking and met them at the course on a bitterly cold early January day. The wind had a nasty bite to it and was of the *cut you into half* variety.

Brian was right into the entire essence of the experience from the start, even though it was perishing cold. Amy tagged along, and despite repeated pleas from me to go back to the cosy refuge of the pavilion, she resolutely stuck with Brian on his wee excursion into golf history. They were a lovely couple who intimated that they intended to come back later in the year when it was a wee bit warmer—well, maybe warmer. This *is* Scotland.

People seemed to be going to extraordinary lengths to sample this modest experience. The Delboys were a father and son duo who came up from London via Red Letter Days and flew up to Scotland on the Friday evening and would be flying back home on the Saturday after their experience!

Ed, the father, turned out to be my nightmare scenario. They were fantastic people, as was the norm, but not everybody got to grips with the unforgiving nature of hickory play. Ed just could not get the hang of getting the ball airborne mostly due to his less than orthodox and rather snappy swing—perfectly fine for the new *game*, but not so for the old *sport*!

I had gone round thirteen holes with them, and Ed hadn't managed to get a single shot off the tee. Every shot was a complete foozle, and he was getting a bit anxious—and so was I! The patter was still good and they were both content with the package, but all my little unqualified tips did nothing to help Ed produce a golf shot.

Dave tried to convince me that his dad normally skelped the ball a mile back home at Wentworth. Of that, I had no doubt because Ed was sturdily built with 'Desperate Dan' shoulders. I had stopped praying for myself a while back, but found myself looking upwards and pleading with Him—to assist Ed in getting, at least, one shot away.

Lo and behold, as we were preparing to play the 5th on the second round, with Dave and I watching in a mindset that anticipated another duff—click, whoooosh, and off the ball went, high and handsome and dead straight in line with the green! The young boomers could reach that green, and here was our Ed on the front edge of it!

By now, Dave and I had gone delirious with joy, and the whole excitement of the occasion was overwhelming. 'I told you, Alfie. Didn't I tell you . . . he could do it!' Dave blasted out. Ed turned to his admiring gallery of two and did not say a word, but displayed the most contented and smug grin I think I've ever witnessed.

The sun was shining again—even though it wasn't, and I'm sure that if one of us had been carrying a hip flask, we would have drunk it dry in celebration. The three of us walked up the fifth hole like we were walking straight into heaven. What fun, spirit, camaraderie, elation—and all for the sake of hitting a wee white ba' roond a glorified field! Golf—what a sport!

The essence of tourism is in having the ability to attract. Nae attractions—nae tourists. There could be no doubt in the fact that Harry and I had built an attraction. Ed and Dave had come to Scotland for hickory golf. Their tourism pounds had been spent on air flights, car hire, hotel, golf, and probably some tartan tat to take home to the family.

They may even have discovered Scotland to be a marvellous destination and made that most desirable act for a tourist—the return visit! I don't know if they have or not. What I do know is that I usually took some pictures so that I could forward them on to the customers after their visit.

Dave and Ed insisted on having me in the mugshots too, and when they were eventually developed, I got the shock of my life. It wasn't me standing next to them. It was some gaunt and ghostly character who looked like he had one foot in the grave. A dead man walking! This just couldn't go on.

We didn't have too many members at Arbory, even though we burst a gut to encourage locals in the area to use the course at bargain basement prices, including the kids with *their* free ticket. One highly valued member we did have was retired banker Mr Davy Syme and his wife, Anna. Davy, a lifetime golfer, was never slow to remind me that he was a past winner of the prestigious 'Silver Tassie' amateur tournament played annually at Carnoustie.

He was a sprightly ninety-year-old, or thereabouts, when he first showed face and intimated his support for our wee venture at Arbory, long before we'd reached the paying customer stage. Davy was still quite a tall and upright man at around six feet with minimal sign of any old age crouching. Obviously, a life in the banking profession had done him little or no physical damage during his lifetime.

If only we could find another hundred like Davy, then the future would look very bright indeed! I remember one fine spring day Anna brought Davy over to the course for a wee hit about. I had been forewarned of the visit and was somewhat apprehensive about taking Davy up on to the course.

The first hole was quite a steep climb for 207 yards and a rude awakening for any golfer who hadn't played there before. Much of the route included some soft marshy ground which was often quite slippery underfoot! Christ, this wasn't a good idea, because I'd already seen much younger men, in their mere seventies, having trouble with that first hole.

No! What I had to do was coax Davy into playing some shots at the bottom of the course where the terrain was much more amiable and easier going on the feet . . . not to mention the heart.

Anna duly arrived at the car park to drop off her excited passenger. 'Are ye fit?' I asked.

'Oh aye, ah cannae wait tae get gaun,' Davy replied while Anna drove off to do some shopping, I think.

'Dae ye fancy a wee cup o' tea afore we start, Davy?'

'Naw, naw. We can do that efter oor gem,' he replied.

Hmmm. I made the suggestion, or was it a plea? 'Ah was thinkin' it might be better to play along the bottom holes, Davy . . . It's a helluva climb up the first, and it can be really slippery as well.'

'Och, ah'll manage fine. It's no' that far' he insisted.

So we doddled our way up to the first tee, reminiscing of the day when the legendary John Panton, one of Scotland's finest pros and Ryder Cup player and captain, made a visit to wee Arbory and played a couple of holes. And on the lower slopes, I must stress!

John had struck a fine shot up the eighth with a brassie and impatiently made after it, leaving the rest of the party on the tee, including Davy. He had taken about ten steps when he turned to Harry and I and said, '*This is excellent turf—it's so springy underfoot!*' That was reassuring to hear that from one of Scotland's finest exponents of the game, and it was evidently clear that Davy was highly chuffed with the company of John Panton too.

'OK then, Davy. There's the green up there. Can ye see it?' I said with a laugh.

'Cheeky bugger. Where do I aim for?' I pointed to a white marker post about 100 yards distant and demanded that he clear the ditch that lay in that proximity, which drew a challenging glare. He took a couple of practice swings and let rip . . . Well, that's to say that he gave it every ounce that he had to offer with the mental determination of a teenager, countered by the physical ability of an adamant nonagenarian!

Bloody hell! He did clear the ditch and pleasingly looked me in the eye and asked, 'Will that do, Alfie?' I don't know who was more chuffed with his accomplishment, him or me, but for me, this was a case of so far, so good, and we hadn't even left the teeing ground yet.

We started to make our way up the fairway (what fairway?) and crossed the sleeper bridge at the ditch without incident, but I did notice that he was blowing quite hard. 'Take yer time, Davy. We've got all day,'

I said. He just gave a wave of his arm and approached his ball. I was sensing stress in my elderly friend, and I was getting anxious for him.

A couple of duffs advanced the ball by fifteen or twenty yards, and the joint elation of the drive minutes earlier disappeared into the mists of golfing aspirations. A good chip shot saw him make the edge of the tiny green, but he was noticeably rocking on his feet! I offered my arm to help him ascend the last ten yards towards flatter land.

The fact is that not only did he accept my offer he also nearly pulled my bloody arm out of its socket in the process. Still, we made it to the green and the conventional two putts were taken as I tended the pin, giving him a commendable six, considering the couple of duffs he had taken.

We shook hands as was customary and right, traded reciprocating smiles, with his showing a hint of distress. Fortunately, Harry and I had planned for such occasions by erecting small bench seats all around the course—little wooden sparred havens of respite which we used frequently ourselves! This one, just above the second tee, had been deliberately designated priority in building order.

I ushered Davy over for a well-earned seat and concealed my sigh of relief full in the knowledge that we still had to get back down to the pavilion. Davy was looking and sounding more composed again, and so was I, after I lit up. We sat and talked golf for about thirty minutes while I consciously held my tongue and used it only to fuel Davy's when his dried up.

I reminded him of the day that he and Anna had walked into a meeting I was having with two of the Enterprise people. It was quite funny and unexpected. When I told Davy, an ex-banker, who the people were, he ripped into them without hesitation! I remember just sitting back and enjoying wholeheartedly Davy's sincere rant.

'And why not give this place some support? Have you looked around the village? We don't have a lot happening here and the work these boys have put in would put other projects to shame, but you'll give money to them, no doubt!' And he went on with the rant till Anna pulled him by the sleeve, and they made for home, promising to come back later. I had one helluva job trying to convince the reps that it hadn't been a set-up and that it was just by pure chance that they'd come in.

This day was not for me; it was for Davy, and I knew that from the start. His golfing game was fast running out of shots, but his mind was bright and he still had all his personal golf nostalgia to fall back on, and there was plenty of it. I heard it all—his decades of playing golf at Lanark and Leadhills as a member, his best moments as a player, the great players he had seen at Open Championships—his golfing life in only thirty minutes or so. I think I had done him a great favour that day, while nearly bloody killing him!

I've never been a fan of electric buggies—*'golf is a walking game'*—but I wish I'd had one for Davy the day we went up the first! He could have played more shots with relative ease and comfort while being able to see, or play, the entire nine holes.

'Are ye fit and ready for going back down, Davy?'

'Aye. Ah suppose so. I don't think it would be very wise to go along the second?' he asked.

'Eh . . . naw. I think a wee cup of tea is required, and when we get down to the good grass, maybe you could try a couple of chips on to the ninth green with a niblick on our way to the pavilion.'

'Good idea. And wi a couple of those old gutty balls. Let's go, Alfie. It should be a wee bit easier going down, eh?'

We slowly descended the same way as we'd come up, through the boggy area, and crossed the ditch to the better firm grass, where I blew a secretive sigh of relief. He played a few chips on to the tiny ninth green and then putted a couple of them out. You'd have thought he was putting for the Open title, such was his determination to sink them! We went into the pavilion, where I instantly put the kettle on. We then sat for about an hour and once more blethered away about golf in some form or another. Anna faithfully arrived to take him home, just a mile across the Clyde. I waved them away in the car park . . . and never saw Mr Davy Syme again. I sincerely hope that he's found golf's Elysian fields upstairs.

Around the same time in the late spring of 2003, I was getting really desperate, full in the knowledge that I had to make a decision one way or another. But I never seemed to give up all hope. Christ! I just didn't know when or how to lie down and let this dream die.

Kevin Pilley, a long-standing friend and stalwart ally, was still churning out articles for SAGA and airline magazines to assist the cause, while I continued to approach the business angels, funding sources, and the political hypocrites of the day, those people who are supposed to run the country, but have no influence. Bullshit!

All sorts of doubts were circulating through my brain in an effort to find some solution to the inevitable failure staring me in the face. The complex equation of life had me dumbfounded. I had feared failure all my life and I had generally treaded a careful line in order to avoid such occurrences. Maybe my own head *was* stuck firmly up my arse, and all this self-belief in an insignificant enterprise had all been a pipe dream from the very start.

And yet so many people were getting back in touch with their letters and emails of support. Were they the true humanitarians that I believe is a crucial ingredient to the essence of golf or was I just romanticising the dream?

Whatever! Life's too short. Yer a long time deid! But no matter what your afflictions or grievances with life, there are always other people who are much worse off than yourself. We shouldn't forget that. But I think most of us . . . do!

Then I opened my Sunday broadsheet to discover a big spread in one of Scotland's most successful entrepreneurs. This guy had made his money and was now in the process of trying to follow in Andra Carnegie's footsteps with his own programme of Scottish philanthropy! Having amassed his fortune in America through his industrial empire, Carnegie set about distributing his wealth in his own belief that '*the man who dies rich, dies disgraced*'. Can't knock the man for that!

The article appeared to be saying all the right things to encourage new businesses within Scotland but also had a strong leaning towards the youth of our great nation. Hmmm, maybe this is the one for me? I think he's a bit of a golfer too. Surely they intend to invest in the middle-aged group as well as the young guns of enterprise? Oh well. We won't know if we don't try, will we?

So the keyboard got slapped about once more and the latest appeal drafted in the utmost haste. Time was of the essence and a package was sent off to a distant flag fluttering away on the west coast of Scotland. It was most probably my final encounter with every golfer's eternal faith in any outcome . . . hope?

Hoping that the weather will be fine today, that the ball doesn't bounce out of bounds, that the ball will carry over the water hazard or bunker, that I won't miss that three foot putt—yes, a golfer's life is embraced in everlasting hope.

Meanwhile, young Craig at the *Gazette* was keeping a close eye on Arbory for any developments and some happy story to report. I had serious doubts of being the bearer of good tidings since I'd already warned Red Letter Days that I was going to have to call a halt to the hickory show.

Naturally, they weren't too pleased, so I asked if they would be interested in making an investment in WHGL Ltd to allow me to keep trading. Understandably, it was against their company policy to get involved with any of the attractions on their books. So that little ploy was a total non-starter.

Time was marching on, and I struggled into May taking the last few bookings I had committed to, pickin' shit and cutting the greens when required. I'd also cancelled a group of ten Americans who had wanted to visit late summer! Bit by bit, I was winding the whole thing down and I still hadn't heard a squeak from the west coast.

Craig phoned to get the latest, and I told him it was all but over and thanked him for the *Gazette*'s support over the last few years. I also told him of my last gambit and how I didn't expect anything to come out of it. He asked if he could contact them and I told him he could. Who knows, maybe it would stir them into action?

I just had enough funds left in the overdraft to enable me to pay back all the vouchers I had sold, and any other outstanding bills were paid off. So I was happy in the knowledge that nobody else was going to lose a penny out of my failings! *A good conscience fears nothing*, as Queen Bessie's saying goes. All I had to do now was arrange a loan with my trusty caring bank to pay off the ten grand overdraft I owed them. Then Craig phoned me back with some breaking news!

'Hi, Alfie. I thought I'd better give you a call to see what's happening.'

'Oh. Not a lot, Craig. I've got what they call—a fucked company!' I said. 'And it doesn't look like the west coast angels are coming on their white horse to save the day either.'

'Oh, I gave them a call, Alfie, and it's not good news,' he said rather sheepishly.

'What do you mean, Craig?'

'Well, they told me they wouldn't be investing in the project. They said they weren't interested.'

'What!' I exclaimed, as Craig started trying to make an apology for being the conveyer of bad news. 'Listen, Craig, don't you worry about that. It's not your fault the bastards didn't have the decency to contact me first. And they're the ones who are supposed to be professional! Inconsiderate bastards!'

The Alfie volcano was preparing for an eruption, and as there was no good news to be conveyed either way, the call was wound up rather swiftly, and I sat alone in the pavilion, juggling with my deepest thoughts.

I soon came to the dismal conclusion. 'That's it then. It's all over, Alfie boy,' I mumbled to the wall and our wee gallery of Clydesdale's defunct golf courses and clubs of yesteryears. Abington was officially defunct—again! There was going to be a lot of crap to tidy up—but not before I vented my disgust at the entrepreneurial professionals who had just shit on me. I never forgot my beloved mother's words of advice at an early age in life: '*Never let anybody shit on ye, Son. Don't ever let them get away with it!*'

As soon as I got home that day, I made for the computer and got busy. I didn't miss them and hit the wall, I can tell you. But I never missed those blazers at the R&A or the politicians either. Hell hath no fury—as an Alfie scorned! And it most definitely makes you feel a little bit better at the time, once you get these annoyances off your chest.

Trying to understand why this small business was being treated like an enterprise leper was beyond me. The bloody thing worked. All it needed was a bit more time to grow and the essential financial lifeline. And what an asset to Scotland's golfing portfolio!

Perhaps I was looking for some payback for trying to live the life as a good person, just as mum had taught *all* of us to do. But life doesn't work that way—does it? You don't get payback for being the best you can—you just do it because it's the right thing to do at the time, and then you forget about it!

I don't think the business world whizz-kids could possibly understand such a philosophy in life. A guy from America, Kim Offers, emailed me, wanting a couple of gutta balls. So I sent him a couple with payment details. *Please donate fifteen bucks to any US Cancer Charity.* Hardly good business sense, but then I was done with all that.

Here was I, nothing less than a common beggar, pleading with Scotland's finest for a wee handout—a wannabe socialist mini government that had Kier Hardie turning in his grave, an enterprise system that only wanted to hear about job numbers and see inflated cash-flow projections that amounted to fraudulent lies, and a wannabe Andra Carnegie who talked a great game in Scotland's broadsheets. Aye, dear old Andra, *the man who dedicated his entire life to the extreme epitome of capitalism, then decided he would rather die a socialist.*

That letter must have struck a chord because there was little delay this time around, with a reply that amounted to an apology. That helped me to cool down, and I reciprocated with my own form of apology, which drew a line under the affair—at least, until now. I continued to wind up the business in the ensuing few months and stopped cutting the greens.

It became a real emotional struggle just to go up and check the place out. Anything that was worth salvaging was taken home, and the two kabins I burnt to the ground. They were knackered anyway, rotten and dysfunctional, a bit like our Scottish tourism strategy at the time!

The biggest problem lay in our wee fancy pavilion that stood at the bottom of Arbory Hill, unwanted and desolate, and now a total white elephant and waste of space. Harry and I had built it to stay; it was now immovable and worthless, empty and devoid of any life or mandatory outbreaks of laughter.

We knew the risk when we lined it all out as best we could for the comfort of our punters. I asked Duncan if he wanted it removed immediately, to which he said it wasn't in the way at the moment and that they had no alternate plans for the ground. That was the response I wanted to hear because the pavilion, modest as it was, remained a workable fixed asset which could allow me to start all over if . . . och well, you know what I mean.

Heaven knows why, but as the months rolled past, I kept on plugging away with politicians (or rather, their monkeys) and the funding people. A few irate letters had also been published in *The Scotsman* newspaper pleading my case, but there were no takers. Visits to the course continued, usually accompanied by Ross, and on one occasion, we found the cattle back on the course!

They had destroyed most of the information signs we'd erected at each tee, and cow pats littered the entire place. The soft patches of turf were all deeply cut up by the hooves of heavy traffic, and the place was looking rather sad. 'Ye see, Ross. That's why golfers didna like cattle on their gowf courses!'

I'd even heard that a new project was being considered near St Andrews for . . . a new golf course to be played with hickory clubs. Someone from Fife Enterprise had phoned me to ask about Arbory and whether I thought the hickory concept was feasible as a business. My answers were all positive for '*who it may have concerned*', and I never heard another squeak from them. I couldn't help but wonder how much public money would get ploughed into that.

The best-laid plans o'mice and men, gang aft aglee!

Ach. Let it fuckin' go!

All Balls, but Nae Courage

The hickory golf experience had become a mission in my life with an axe to grind concerning the ongoing technology debate. I could get up on to my soapbox at Arbory to address small groups and individuals and let rip with regard the runaway modern ball!

There was no better place on the planet to *show* every golfer why a rollback of the ball should be implemented by the rule makers. Even better, every player taught themselves as they played round the course with balls that just didn't go as far as they were used to—in modern play. The balancing factor was that they didn't *have* to hit them as far on this course because the *scale* between the ball and the course was fine, just as it should be!

Here was a place in golf where the issues could be discussed openly and freely. No sweeping the ball under the carpet or hiding heads under the sand at this wee golf course. I don't know how many people would say to me at the end of the day, 'I see (understand) what you're going on about now, Alfie!' Not everybody agreed with my opinions, but they all understood the issues much better.

Such was my belief in the futility of allowing the ball to go far that I wrote (not that well) an essay on *the problem* and distributed it to all my contacts around the world. One of my past customers, Paul Lavaroni from the States, showed it to his friend, Sandy (Frank) Tatum, past president of the USGA, who apparently wholeheartedly agreed with its content and presented the essay to the USGA annual meeting a few years back.

When Paul informed me of this, I thought it was only right and proper that I send a copy to the blazers at the R&A at St Andrews out of courtesy. I should have known better and received the following reply by email—there are other opinions on the matter:

That was it! No 'dear sir'; no 'from so or so'; no 'caps or full stop'; no—just piss off and leave us alone, Mr Ward—ya shit stirring bastard! Absolutely shocking, in *my* opinion. Just like the response to our funding appeal.

Who are these people who have the remit to *protect and preserve* our great sport of golf? Shame on them! They can't even bestir themselves to erect a fitting monument to Tom Morris Sr! Don't they realise that *history* will, sooner or later, unveil they're apathetic and cowardly defence of a great sport?

When I played most of my golf from 1970s to 1980s, the game was fine. There wasn't a problem with golf that I, or millions of others, could see. Of course, it would take another book to explain the technology problem in detail, and it doesn't help when certain people don't want to talk about the problem with the modern ball and its negative effects related to lost skill factors, higher maintenance costs for golf courses, far longer time required to play a round, higher costs for the player generally, the architecture of our great (and not so great) courses being overwhelmed and devalued . . .

Shhhhhhhh, there are other opinions on the matter.

Oh dear. *The devil makes work for idle thumbs.* My evenings were now devoid of excessive hours of trying to save the lost cause. No more promotional emails to launch into the futile vacuum of cyberspace and no more administrative work for the running of a business. No more shit pickin' for that matter. I had time on my hands for the first time in years! I had also lost my Arbory platform for waging war on those technology advances and decided to reinstate some research hours.

This was the time when I found Max Behr. Through my contributions to the discussion group at www.golfclubatlas.com, I noticed Behr's name cropping up now and again, and this intrigued my curiosity. Through another protagonist, Geoff Shackleford, I was steered towards the electronic source of Behr's editorials in *Golf Illustrated*.

The more I read Behr's work, the more I became fascinated by him. Here was a man who understood the very essence of the sport and foresaw the problems with the ball at the start of the twentieth century—almost the same problem that exists today, a hundred years on! In 1927, he wrote an essay—'The Ball Problem'—in which he analysed the sport in relation to how golf was being affected by continuing distance advances of the ball at that time.

Incredulously, the ruling bodies have allowed the futile distance war to rage on for more than a century while other sports, more streetwise to protecting *their* respective sports, have shown the manufacturers the door with various attempts at introducing new technologies—bats and balls, for instance!

Personally, I think the issue of club technology is a case of where the genie has been allowed out of the bottle—and the ruling bodies have a task on their hands trying to put the bugger back in! The ball, on the other hand, is a totally different matter, which could be remedied immediately by rolling the technology of the ball back in time to a predetermined point in golf ball history.

Simples! Even the number one blazer at the R&A has quoted on TV that 'this would be a relatively simple matter' (to invoke)! Dissenting voices, especially in the last twenty years, have been calling for such a rollback and represent a who's who from leading professionals, golf course architects, and golf writers. Unfortunately, for golf, they all operate as lone soldiers rather than get themselves really heard by forming an army to fight the cause. Of course, there are other opinions on the matter.

Apologists for the ruling bodies will tell you that there is a risk of litigation from the manufacturers, that it's not so simple to rollback the ball, that there isn't a problem in the first instance, that the average golfer would rebel against such an action, that nothing progresses by taking a step back. Absolute tosh in every point of feeble intransigence!

Wake up and smell the coffee, people. Just smell the coffee! And history will show exactly what the defence of the sport has been for over a century of futility. Ball goes long—put the tees back a few yards until your back is up against the boundary fence or, alternately, build new greens on the far-off horizon till you reach the boundary there. Then, as the ball goes longer and longer, buy more land—if your course is in the countryside.

Meanwhile, some of our *classic* courses such as the Old Course and Augusta National have run out of real estate and now play tee shots from foreign lands in order to compensate the distance problem (what problem?). Our great championships are embarrassed by the desperate defences put up to protect the courses' dignity over ever-improving talent. They narrow the fairways and grow long rough, excavate more bunkers and create water hazards, and trick up the greens to lightning speeds till they become unplayable—think Shinnecock Hills!

Oh, how our administrators (past and present) have embarrassed our sport through inaction and lame excuse making, while they bury their heads in the sand! Shame on them for not having the guts to stand up for the sport and finally quell the pandering instincts of manufacturers who care little for the essence of golf and more for their profit margins! And that's only natural—for them!

And would the few ball manufacturers left in the industry actually contemplate suing our governing bodies over the implementation of a rolled back ball to conform to the rules? Never! They would be mad to tackle the sleeping giants who are their very lifeblood—their own customers who give profit and gain. Anyway, it doesn't matter what kind of ball they make or whether it doesn't go as far. So long as golf remains a pleasurable and desired pastime, the golfers will still need a zillion balls every year!

The whole issue of distance has nothing to do with traditionalists like myself. That's just a coincidence, and if I had my way, there would be rollbacks of the clubs too! Golf's problem (what problem?) lies with those who administer the rules and whether they have the will and courage to rectify a century of misadventure in our sport. It's not too late. Enough is enough!

Behr summed up his essay in the final paragraph of his 'Ball Problem' essay in 1927:

The problem of the ball is the most serious that golf has ever been faced with. It is one that our authorities must solve successfully. And while they are about it, the question before the golfers of the world is plain as a pike-staff. Are they going to be sportsmen and accept a ball that requires skill to propel, or, in their infantile worship of mere distance, are they going to continue to be downright game-hogs?

Dear Max, just in case you didn't know, there are other opinions on the matter! Kindest regards, Alfie & Harry x.

I was commissioned by another enthusiast and friend, Chris (hickory) Homer, to make a batch of guttas for some of his clients. Chris had an oncoming hickory gig in Sweden and wanted the balls to be presented as special gifts for the participants of a special hickory match. I had been trying, unsuccessfully, for some time to procure a supply of good 'raw' natural gutta, in order to make a sideline income from making the old gutta balls of which I had sold quite a number, over the past few years.

I turned to another gutta expert and friend in St Andrews, David Hamilton, from whom I knew I could borrow his 'Challenger' golf ball mould to make the balls. David is the author of many fine golfing books including *Precious Gum*, the story of gutta-percha and golf balls.

David was my last hope for a source of good gutta, but he too was struggling to find this elusive olde worlde material. Instead, he could only advise of a dental company in Switzerland, which would supply a 'form of gutta' which would mould quite well—but could only be used in a practical sense for putting! This wasn't a satisfactory outcome as far as I was concerned—just not 'cricket', my good man.

Golf balls had been made for centuries whether from wood, feathers, gutta-percha, rubber, balata . . . or the scientific crap they make them from nowadays. Regardless of the technology applied, they all had one thing in common—they were there to be given a bloody good whack with a fucked-up stick of some sort.

Ted Ray was a big hitting professional who had won The Open in 1912. When asked by a young man as to how he could achieve greater distance, Ted had replied rather curtly, '*Hit it a bloody sight harder, mate!*'

Advance into a few decades and the legendary Arnie Palmer was once asked what his thoughts were when he struck a golf ball, '*Gee. I just tee that little white ball up, and think, "Hell! I'm gonna hit the shit out of you"!*' And that's exactly what he did throughout his illustrious career.

I had a dilemma! If I went ahead and made these balls with inferior material and for a little financial gain, then I would be selling the sport short just like the R&A had done with their ineptitude at controlling the modern ball! Those balls would be nothing more than bloody ornaments for punters' desktops. I don't do ornaments. Royal Doulton do bloody ornaments!

But at the end of the day, I was skint, and so there was no room for moral ethics when it came down to putting some grub on the table. So I made a batch of around 100 ornamental gutta balls with David's authentic 'Challenger' mould and haven't made another one since!

There was no way on earth that I was about to give up entirely on 'the dream'. Through the discussion group at www.golfclubatlas.com, I became friendly with Mark Rowlinson, author of the *World Atlas of Golf* and a fine baritone chanter. Mark had intimated his desire to meet up and have a go at hickory golf, since he was going to be up in Scotland at a gig with the Scottish Philharmonic Orchestra. Although I no longer had my Arbory Braes playground, I had come up with a contingency plan that was befitting of a hickory golfing experience.

Leadhills golf course is situated high up in the Lowther hills about seven miles from Abington, and the course is seldom busy with people. Similar to all that sits around this past lead mining village, the entire place is a tranquil and quaint living time capsule of a small village of yesteryears.

Golf had begun here in 1891 with nine holes laid out on the Broadlaw hill, which sat above the present day course. At one time, the two courses were amalgamated into eighteen before they decided to stick with nine on the lower ground and abandon the original course. The tees and greens of the original course are still visible today, because they were cut out of the Broadlaw hillside.

Mark duly arrived at the course, and we played around the course with hickories and gutta with me 'going into one' as we strolled along the way. Mark took photos as we progressed with a view to posting a feature on the golfclubatlas web site which is still online to this day—Leadhills and the joys of gutta-percha.

When we had finished with our golf, I suggested he could follow me back down to the main road but that we would go via Crawford, where I would show him where the defunct course was situated there. This we did, with Mark appearing to be quite fascinated with this mini tour of Clydesdale.

As we prepared to get back into the cars and head off again, I asked Mark if he would like to see where Arbory Braes lay dormant before getting him back on to the motorway. Again, he agreed, and again he followed me along the back road to Abington, where I took him past the houses on the main street and stopped at a convenient gap in the roadside trees. We were only about half a mile from the course 'as the crow flies', looking over the railway line and River Clyde with Arbory Hill rising against the skyline, but this was close enough for me.

I pointed at the course and explained the layout, from that safe distance. Mark looked at me rather bemused by why we should stop here and not at the course itself. 'Is it all right to go over to the course and walk over it, Alfie?' Mark enquired.

'Oh yes! Not a problem in the slightest, Mark. If you do a U-turn and follow the road keeping left, you'll come to it and you can't get lost. But I'm afraid I can't come with you this time.'

Mark was still looking a bit bemused and pressed the question, 'Why not, Alfie?'

I gave a sigh and said, 'Oh well, it's been a wee while since I was last up here, Mark, and I'm still trying to learn how to . . . let it go. I just don't feel ready to go back over there, Mark. Memories and all that. But I will one day . . . with Harry!'

Mark gave an approving nod, and we bade each other farewell. Mark did go over to the course and walked over it, and a few weeks later, he posted the feature of his day out at Leadhills with gutta-percha on gca. com. I made for home, thinking that maybe there was still some kind of future for hickory golf.

I don't know why I was continuing to flog this dead horse, but I was. I took a few small groups over the ancient 'Old' Musselburgh course near Edinburgh—a place which, in my estimation, could easily claim that title of being 'The hame O' gowf'! This is where, in 1885, the 'brassie' was invented due to the players slicing their shots on to the main road running parallel with the course and them having to play off the road.

A brass plate was inserted on the sole of the club to protect it from such shots. Some of the earliest celebrities of golf came from Musselburgh. The Parks, the Dunns, Bob Ferguson, David Brown, Jamie Anderson, and Willie Campbell were all born here and were Open Champions at one time or another.

John Gourlay and his family became renowned as being the most adept at making the feathery golf balls while all the aforementioned would further the evolution of the sport through inventions, club and ball making, course architecture, and taking the sport to the Americas.

The course hosted six of the early Open Championships and was bestowed the title 'Royal' Musselburgh in 1876. The hole in golf had always been something of a random affair until the R&A standardised the size of the hole to four and a quarter inches in 1893—the same size as the cutting implement that had been used at Musselburgh Links for decades. Before the hole cutters came into being, it has been suggested that the green-keeper used his clenched fist as a gauge to cut round with a knife and form a new hole. Any clenched fist measures approximately four and a quarter inches.

Incredulously, plans were well under way to develop the race track which shared this hallowed turf with the golf course. These proposals would have decimated the most historic piece of golfing turf in the world, possibly dating back to as early as 1567 when Mary, Queen of Scots, is thought to have played here before she lost that essential eye contact with the ball. Thankfully, after much protestation from locals and some outside influence, the plans were scuppered. Anyway, I wanted to use this place for my new brand of hickory play which was more important than some fancy race track.

One such group was mustered up by a golfclubatlas friend from London, Tony Muldoon. A real international blend of about ten inquisitive golfers, who were mostly contributors to the web site, they all played round in good weather, and I '*jockeyed*' back and forth between the groups, giving them as much information as I could.

The gig was fine with everybody enjoying the occasion, but something was missing. It was Arbory Braes and Harry! Historic turf as it was, Old Musselburgh didn't have the same atmosphere as Arbory. This wasn't home. After the gig, Tony asked me to accompany him along the coast to historic North Berwick, where we walked and chatted over most of the course before I decided it was time for home. A relaxing conclusion to a lovely day, but I knew the building site was waiting to avenge my absence the next day!

Another group I steered round Musselburgh was the adorable Mrs Diane Lewis, her husband, and two friends from Yorkshire. Ross came with me that day, and the weather held up once more. This area on the east coast of Scotland is reputed to have the least annual rainfall in the country, believe it or not. Maybe this was true? . . . Wait! Of course, I know why I've pursued this bloody hickory golf thing so much. It's because of the people. Golf and its wonderful people! I'm glad I finally managed to work that one out. No highbrow and no qualifications, you see!

I'm no literary expert, with not a solitary 'O' level in my possession, so these modest lines may appear badly written to the highbrow dominie of good English. Stuff them! I didn't go to all this trouble for the likes of them. You know the genre—*you didn't dot the 'i's and cross the 't's brigade*. Similar to all that has gone before, this exercise has been done 'on the cheap' in order to simply tell the story and (possibly) see what happens.

Dream on.

Ashes to Ashes

The day had finally arrived. The day I had been dreading for so long now. Closure—that's what some people would call it, but I can't imagine I'll see closure on this little facet of my life till they do the same to me—as I was about to inflict upon our wee pavilion!

I hadn't been near the place for a couple of years although I would always force a glimpse of Arbory's slopes from the M74 a mile distant, while on some southward journey. The last time I'd paid a visit was to strip off the tin roof to use on a friend's garage roof. Salvage!

Only temporary planning permission had been granted when we erected our small pavilion. Time was well up and the planners wanted the pavilion removed, and quite rightly so as it had been attended to by the usual scum who had made their vandalistic mark on its defenceless presence.

It was entirely made of timber, apart from the foundations that Harry and I had built in most hellish weather. A gallon of petrol and some papers would suffice for its permanent removal.

I got there about eleven in the morning and found the weather to be calm and pleasant. Generally, Coldchapel road is a minor back road and usually very quiet and bereft of people or traffic. Good, there's nobody lurking about. I had a look inside at what once was modest but immaculate and found a sorry sight.

The scum had been busy doing the only thing their mentality can cope with—destroying other people's property. I had to get out pretty fast—the hyperventilating had begun. The 7th and 9th greens lay only yards away, so I meandered my way over to inspect them which would serve to distract my mind from the inevitable.

Greens! What greens? All that work we had put into getting them right for the job was gone. Hard even to imagine that we had been there at all. She's a hard bitch, old Mother Nature! There was no point in pursuing further punishment in this area, so I headed back to the main job in hand.

I don't know why I was stalling, but I was. Old Tom Morris is hardly likely to jump over the fence and stop this arsonous deed, is he? This ain't gettin' the job done, Alfie. It was time to warm the atmosphere around Arbory Braes.

I went to the car to get the arsonist's tools of trade—the petrol and newspapers, and took them into the pavilion. I must have reminisced for another ten minutes or so before I gave a couple of the walls a good dousing and set some papers on the floor, being wary not to get foolishly caught out here.

Ironically, this was a time for me to be careful, right? I recalled being bloody stupid in my younger years when I tried to get an almost dead fire going by pouring petrol straight from the can on to the smouldering embers. Whoooosh! How I wasn't badly burnt I'll never know—but I did lose my nasal hair, my eyebrows, and the first couple of inches of my hairline, and I can remember that stench of burning hair!

Looking around me, I began to see all 'her' ghosts. Neil and I chatting on the bench seat that Ronnie had made and supping a bottle of Neil's slow gin till midnight. Harry busy wiring all the switches and sockets. Pat and Michael installing the gas hot water heater. Colin, Michael, and Jim doing our plumbing for us. All free of charge to help us along the way. The bemused customers as I brought them soft gutta to roll their own golf ball and the priceless expressions on their faces. Jim Dodson and Patrick listening to me sermonise the sinking ship. There were so many other thoughts coming and going in little flashbacks of memory.

Do it! Just fuckin' do it!

I looked out the window towards the new caravan park half a mile away, to see if anyone was going about and heading in this direction. Eyes glazed and dripping, I flicked on the lighter to a flame and lit the rolled paper that I had in my hand and which I could barely see for tears—and I tossed it at the wall and the pile of papers on the floor. No messing, off it went with the 'whooosh' previously mentioned, and flames instantly began spiralling up and along the ceiling just over the top of my head as I stood there momentarily in a daze. Better get the hell out of here, pal. No going back now. Time to 'let it go', hmm?

Outside, the smoke started to billow from the patio and main door, and I could hear the interior pine cladding beginning to crackle in protest. I checked out the time . . . high noon! Not much I can do now; might as well have a fag then. But my hands were shaking uncontrollably, and it was difficult to light the bloody thing.

Christ! The smoke was intense, and I hadn't seen this much since Harry and I burnt off the dried out and dead rushes on the course. Harry? Aye, better that he hasn't seen this. I'm consciously thinking of him and really glad that he isn't here to share in the cremation of our dream.

About six or seven minutes had elapsed before the flames broke free from within and started to swallow up and engulf the roof. Oh dear, I hope some silly bugger in the village doesn't go and phone the fire brigade. Not that they could have done anything. This process was a one-way exhibition to simulate hell. I was beginning to calm down when I noticed a large group heading down the road towards me. Aw shit, who's this coming? It turned out to be a class of school children from the local primary and two of their teachers.

The kids started to run towards this exciting and unexpected attraction, and I had to step in and tell the little buggers to keep back. As the two teachers approached, they both called me by name, but I still couldn't place them as to who they were. They probably knew me from when my daughter, Kelly, assisted at the school.

A hill walker from the Kilmarnock area also appeared, and it was becoming quite a gathering. Tea, coffee, and soft drinks could have made me a few bob. One of the lady teachers exclaimed, 'Are you bringing in the new year early, Alfie?' It was a reference to the annual Biggar Hogmanay bonfire which is quite a spectacle each New Year. I hesitated with my response for a few seconds, then saw the funny side of her comment. How was she to know what had preceded her arrival.

'Not quite,' I retorted. 'But if you haven't seen it before—this is how a dream burns!'

None of them hung about for long. Maybe they'd detected my vibes of disappointment and disconsolation. I was on my own again—just me, my thoughts, and a burning pavilion raising ashen memories high into the clear blue sky above.

Bastards! Where are they now? Perhaps I should have invited a few of them along to see this spectacle? Ah well, no point in being bitter, is there? Visionless political and entrepreneurial . . . rascals.

Forty-five minutes had gone and it was still resisting. A few studs remained charcoaled and upright, reminiscent of the tragic 911 World Tower (incomparable, of course), and I had to push them over with a stick into the remnants of the fire. I could see the block work foundations that Harry and I had jointly built in cold miserable weather starting to appear through what was left of the charcoaled floor.

I could remember Harry's self-contentment in building his first few concrete blocks. A simple fascination of labour mysteriously enjoyed by so many, like Winston Churchill for example, but unsurprisingly, seldom enjoyed so industriously by the brickie himself!

By now, the show was almost over, and it was just a case of seeing the final embers die out to a safe standard and then tidy up the bits and pieces that had somehow fallen around the perimeter of the building. I had done my bit, and there was no sign of blood on my hands, just soot. Duncan would see to the concrete foundations with a digger machine if they posed a problem to the planners. Fait accompli!

On the drive home, I felt like a huge burden had been left behind, and yet there was no sense of relief. It was a dirty job, but somebody had to do it! I recalled Harry's fateful words, 'Ye cannae dae all this work without something good coming out of it!' It didn't seem to matter how many good turns you had done in your life for organisations or people who 'needed' a wee turn to help them out—life simply didn't work . . . Harry's way! I knew within myself that I still hadn't learnt to . . . let it go.

I never did see any phoenix rise from the ashes!

Never Say Never. The Chase Goes On!

After I had finally pulled the plug on our field of dreams, I found my life, in many ways, empty and devoid of any hopes and aspirations. When conversing with people in post-mortem fashion about my Arbory emotions, some would continue to utter the old cliché, 'You have to learn to let it go, Alfie.'

Hell no! Why should I? I still maintained one hundred per cent faith and belief in the entire project with the hindsight of recognising the many innocent mistakes Harry and I had made throughout the journey and not forgetting the dramatic misfortunes that befell us! Let it go? That'll be right! I never did get my head round that expression—and still haven't!

I still had in my possession thirteen sets of hickories and a good stock of gutty golf balls, and most importantly, the passion and enthusiasm remained firmly intact for the entertaining of inquisitive golfers who would desire a day with golf history and me.

The same old problem was haunting me though. 'The erse was hingin' oot ma trousers', as we say in Scotland for one being financially disadvantaged. I was paying off the £10,000 overdraft I had accumulated up to the point of pulling the plug on Arbory and would be doing so for a few years to come! I was bloody skint and still couldn't advertise myself properly.

However, there remained just a glimmer of hope because most of the Internet providers facilitated free web pages for their customers. Generally, they were crap and merely an enticement to get people to buy marketing expertise once you were signed up. But they were free, and any web presence with advertising and exposure was better than none at all! So I began setting up a few web pages and the adrenalin flowed once more through the veins, albeit a trickle in comparison to our previous exploits.

Around the same time in September 2004, an interesting development happened in my life. No, not another woman—that would come later! I was sitting watching the telly one night when an advert jumped out of the TV and bit me on the nose! It was none other than the Department of Employment touting for wannabe entrepreneurs with a brand new 'scheme' aimed at getting unemployed unfortunates off their lazy arses and getting themselves into the big business world.

Fame, fortune, and untold happiness awaited those who ventured into and enrolled with NEW DEAL! 'C'mon. You can do it!' was their appeal slogan. That'll do for me, I thought. I can do it. I've done it. This could work for me at last . . . maybe? Nothing ventured, nothing gained.

The next morning, I phoned to set up a meeting for 'New Deal' at the Lanark office for the unemployed. A day or two later, I ventured forth to a place which had become familiar territory over the years for different reasons. Entering the building, I knew exactly where I was going—and exactly where I didn't want to go. Up the stairs to the first floor where an element of the scum got their handouts from the Social Security Department and where Ross and I had encountered some scum on a previous mission some months earlier.

The Social Security pundits had been hounding me for several months (totally unjustified, I must add) over an alleged indiscretion in my business accounts. They summoned me into scumland to try and sort out the alleged indiscretion, and Ross just happened to be with me that day.

When we went into the room, there was an elderly man sitting, waiting his turn for service. There were three positions for interviews to be conducted by the staff sitting safely behind toughened security glass! The kind of place where decent folk might be forgiven for thinking, 'What the fuck am I doing in here?'

Such places also have their procedures, and in this case you were supposed to ring the bell for attention and wait. One of the staff came through into the cages, and the old gent duly stepped forward to talk to her about his business. Ross and I sat patiently after ringing the bell while wondering what the hell were we doing in this place. They say that timing is everything. Well, as fate would have it, just as the old guy was nearing the end of his interview a scumbag and his female scumbag partner entered the room and galloped up to the booth where the old guy was just getting to his feet in order to leave.

They nearly knocked him over in the rush to get his vacant seat, disregarding the fact that Ross and I were waiting our turn! And that was like a red rag to a bull as far as I was concerned. 'Hey, arsehole! Ye ring the bell and wait yer turn!' I exclaimed in diplomatic and courteous fashion.

At the first instance, he and his partner declined my invitation to remove themselves from the booth and allow me to take my rightful turn. 'Fuck off!' was his indignant response. Oh well, when diplomacy fails, the sword is mightier than the tongue, methinks.

I walked into the booth, pointing at the woman behind the security glass. 'Don't bother serving him—he's just going out to wait his turn. I've been waiting here for twenty minutes!'

At this point, she instantly jumped out of her seat and ran into the staffroom, shouting, 'Fight! Fight! There's going to be a fight!'

I was now standing over this little scumbag bastard with my six-foot-two-inch frame flexed and ready for action. I looked him straight in the eye with mine at popping point. 'Well?' I shouted. 'Either you get out and wait yer turn, or I'll drag ye out and throw ye doon the fuckin' stairs fur good measure!'

That seemed to do the trick because he obediently rose and vacated the seat, with his partner defiantly remonstrating at me all the time. I think Ross was quietly impressed with his old dad's conduct and was ready for back-up if required. It wasn't, and we left the building after about thirty minutes of inquisition, cleared of all charges and not an apology in sight!

No, I certainly don't want to revisit scumland. Of my many weaknesses—I'm an intolerant big bastard, especially when dealing with the scum you happen across now and then! I often refer to the Hingin' judge from Dundee who had a bit of a reputation a few centuries back.

A young offender had been brought before him for stealing an apple, and the judge caused a public outcry when he sentenced the boy to death for his crime! The young lad escaped the gallows after furious public protest, and the judge was asked to explain his actions. '*Well!*' he said. '*Hing a thief when he's young—and he'll no steal when he's auld!*' was his judicious reply. Before the days of political correctness, of course!

On passing the SS door, I couldn't resist a little snigger at the nostalgic memories of that place. Onwards and upwards I went to the other place which is more geared up for those who actually want a job or perhaps a new deal.

The place had changed quite considerably since my previous visit and looked more high-tech and modern than it had been before. I approached the reception point to advise of my arrival and was told that I should take a seat in the area behind me and that someone would come and see me.

As I turned and looked round, I felt modestly impressed because New Deal had its own little independent area (just like Scotland should have) and it looked quite welcoming. A very attractive lady made her way towards me and enquired, 'Alfred Ward?'

'Aye. That's me. And it's Alfie,' I replied. She then introduced herself as Caroline, and we sat down in preparation of doing business.

'OK, Alfie. What is it that you have in mind and how do think we can help?' she asked.

I then went 'into one' and started rattling out the sorry story so far and how I thought that New Deal might just give me another chance with hickory golf. After about ten minutes of questions and answers, she said, 'OK, Alfie, I have to ask you some questions and fill in these forms to see if you qualify to register for the scheme.'

'Fire away, Caroline. I'm all ears.'

'Right. Do you have a drink or alcohol problem of any kind?'

'Eh. Well, I used to like a good drink, but I'm teetotal now and a fully paid up member of the Temperance Society,' I said with a grin.

'Have you ever had problems with drugs, either now or in the past?'

'Ehh. Never touched drugs in my life, but I do like ma bacci. Just ordinary Golden Virginia and never the wacky bacci!' This time I gave a laugh.

'I'm sorry, but I do have to ask before we assess if you are eligible for the scheme,' she said with a hint of embarrassment. I was now beginning to see the penny drop, and doubt was creeping into my mind as to whether this new effort with another system was just another waste of time.

'Have you ever been in prison or . . . ?'

I interrupted at this point because I had realised where this line of questioning was heading, and it wasn't amusing me any more, because the outcome seemed inevitable for me.

'Sorry, Caroline, for interrupting, but I hope this isn't leading to a knock-back purely because I'm *not* a violent drunken thief with a drug problem? Please tell me I'm wrong.' This scheme, I was beginning to think, might better be administered downstairs in scumland.

She looked rather puzzled as to what she should do, then after a brief pause, she said, 'Obviously, there's a criteria to follow, and your circumstances don't appear to fall into that criteria . . . and that just doesn't seem fair considering what you've told me about your idea and your present circumstances.' She sat pondering for a minute or so and then rose from her seat. 'Could you excuse me for a few minutes, Alfie? I'm going to talk to my manager about this and see what he thinks.'

'Certainly, Caroline. Take as long as you want,' I replied calmly, although inside I could feel the heat of the Ward volcano building up for an explosion—not aimed at the lovely Caroline, but at the bloody system again! I could see her talking with her boss through a glass screen in his office and turned in my chair now and again just to have a sly keek at what was going on. After almost ten minutes of debate and me keeking over my shoulder, she re-entered the main arena and headed towards me.

'Well, Alfie, I've had a good talk with my boss, and even though you don't really qualify for this scheme, we both agree that you should be allowed on it,' she said with a charming smile but adamant prose. 'There's just a couple of forms to fill in and then I'll explain what happens next,' she continued.

I have to admit my mind was wandering and straying in mischievous mode to matters that had little to do with New Deal! 'I really do appreciate your help, Caroline. Thanks.'

'Not at all. That's what I'm here for.'

So we got the paperwork out of the way, and then she explained that I would have to attend meetings every week initially with a business councillor in Motherwell called Gerry O'Donnell–about an hour in the car from my home in Biggar. I would also have to report back to Caroline every now and again with progress reports of how things were shaping up. Oh my, that was going to be a hardship.

Off I went to Motherwell a few days later, fully armed with old leftover leaflets and brochures, photographs, the visitors' book with all its customer comments, the original business plan, and a whole load of other stuff with, just for good measure, a set of hickories and some gutta and gutty balls thrown into the boot of the car.

I really didn't have a clue whether this new exercise was going to throw up some kind of result or whether it would be more of the same old time-wasting crap that I'd grown accustomed to. As I drove along, my thoughts juggled from positive to negative, negative to positive, and wondered what this Gerry guy was going to be like. Will I like him or will he be another prat?

Chances are, I thought, he'll never have hit a golf ball in his life and could even turn out to be one of the many golf haters. Oh well, just have to find his place of work and I'll soon have all the answers.

I found the office and made my introduction to the receptionist who told me Gerry would be with me in a minute or two. Sure enough, he appeared and introduced himself in a professional manner. He was slightly on the portly side and appeared quite cheery as he ushered me into a private office.

'Right then, Alfie. Caroline's been telling me all about yourself and your project that didn't quite work out for you. That was a pity–I had a failed business too, you know.' Always having a tendency of being pre-judgemental towards people I've just met, I immediately took to Gerry and felt comfortable with his company. I just nodded and smiled as he explained some procedural details. I would get an hour of his time before his next candidate appeared.

'OK, Alfie. First of all, how do you fancy telling me about your wee golf course and what you think went wrong with it?'

Feelings of déjà vu tickled my nerve endings at his invitation for me to . . . 'go into one' regarding Arbory. Here I go again. Better forewarn Gerry of the big yin blabbin' away about golf and its history. 'No problem, Gerry. But if you get bored, just put your hand up and I'll stop,' I jested.

And then . . . I went into one . . . for at least half an hour with Gerry making short intermittent comments, sometimes shaking his head, nodding in approval, generally giving me my platform for him to make some kind of assessment. I was in my element for the first time in a long, long while, and I was at ease with myself and I suppose—my inner ego.

It was the time and opportunity to get a whole load of crap off my chest, which had been festering there for too long. A little golf history lesson followed by the nuts and bolts of the business concept Harry and I had pinned all our hopes upon. Gerry was a self-confessed . . . non-golfer!

Maybe this would just be another waste of breath and time. On I went in blethering mode till the blood began to warm just before reaching boiling point and the final lambasting of . . . those bastards who could have thrown us some kind of lifeline! 'I tried them all, Gerry. The great socialist leaders of Scotland in their wee kiddie-on parliament. McLeish, Alexander, Finnie, Fagan, and a certain hellraiser to whom the great bard would have declared:

> ye see yon birky ca'd a lord,
> wha struts and stares and a' that.
> Tho' hundreds worship at his word,
> He's but a cuif for a' that!'

I had gone through them all like a dose of salts and felt all the better for it! Call it spite, anger, frustration, bitterness, I had my little tantrum whether Gerry wanted to hear it or not. And then I stopped for breath and just looked Gerry in the eye, giving a wry smile and shrug of the shoulders.

Gerry looked back in silence and then threw his pencil rather angrily on to his desk, almost as in a show of disgust. I began to think that I had, perhaps, offended him in some way.

He then swung his swivelling office chair to ninety degrees, leant back, and threw his feet up on to a small cabinet (perhaps in relaxation from his ordeal of listening to me for thirty to forty minutes?). 'I don't understand, Alfie. I just don't get it!' He was apparently speaking to the wall, reminiscent of myself after Craig's ill-fated phone call.

I kept my silence, patiently waiting for him to turn back to face me and give some professional appraisal . . . or something. 'Why did this business fail? I'm not a golfer, but I think the whole idea was marvellous. I just don't fuckin' get it,' he protested.

Hmm. Gerry was a guy who let the occasional oath blurt out now and again. This was good. I like that in men! Personally, I swear like the proverbial 'trooper' but always try to watch my language in front of the ladies and children. The old ministers of long ago attained a reputation frowned upon for letting the odd oath rip after a bad shot on the course, and many a joke was made as a result of their weakness:

> A young minister was learning to play golf, but making a very poor attempt of it. He was seen grinding his teeth and looking as though he would like to say something.
>
> 'Oot wi' it, maister,' said the caddie. 'Oot wi' it, for ye'll never learn if ye dinnae.'

The chair swung back and Gerry was face to face with me again. 'Have you heard of a guy called Satty Singh, Alfie?'

'Nah. Can't say that I have, Gerry,' I replied.

'Well, he's a very successful businessman in Glasgow. He owns several curry houses and they call him the Curry King.'

I was bemused and wondered what relevance all this regal curry had to do with me.

Gerry continued, 'He's just invested in the golf academy at Newton Mearns on the south side of Glasgow, and I think he might be interested in what you have to offer. Would you like me to set up a meeting for you?'

Well, bugger me! The positivity was bursting through my veins and arteries at the prospect of some semblance of a hickory revival—of some description. After all, I could take my business to any course on the planet and give a good historical golf experience to anyone who wanted it.

'Aye! Of course, Gerry. Do you know him?' I enquired curiously.

'Ah know everybody!' he said boldly and with a hint of jovial arrogance.

We both smiled, and he started filtering through his mobile contacts for Satty's number and duly found it. 'I hope this is still his mobile number, Alfie.'

Sure enough it was, and I sat and listened to an old pals' conversation before Gerry got down to the business in hand—of getting me a meeting at Newton Mearns. 'Alfie's sitting here with me right now. I'll just ask him . . . Can you make Thursday morning about ten, Alfie?'

'Aye. No problem, Gerry,' I replied without hesitation.

Any apprehensions from an hour earlier had dissipated into the realms of negativity land. I was feeling heartened and optimistic again. My new-found friend had done the business for me, and now it would be up to me to convince Mr Satty Singh of a hickory golf experience at *his* golf course and academy.

Gerry looked at his watch and declared that his next client was due in five minutes and that we'd have to wind up our tête-à-tête for the time being. Another meeting at Motherwell was arranged for a week later, when I would be able to report on any developments at Newton Mearns.

'All that talkin' has left me gaspin' for a fag, Gerry,' I retorted.

'Aye. Me too, Alfie. Don't run away. I'll see you outside.'

Not only was Gerry another dirty smoker but he also rolled his own like me. And so we spent another five or ten minutes outside puffing our Golden Virginia amid more general conversation before Gerry went back inside and I headed for home.

I can remember the sun shining brightly that afternoon, and my Rod Stewart tape got big licks on the journey home to Biggar. The brain was going into overdrive planning a strategy for the forthcoming meeting at Newton Mearns. My biggest concern was how the bloody hell would I get there.

I must be the worst navigator on the planet. I can get lost in my hometown of Biggar, if I stray away from the main street. Glasgow and its surrounding suburbs with all their one-way systems and roundabouts send shivers down my spine, whenever I have to find a destination point in this area of Scotland!

RAC route finder at the ready, I headed off for Newton Mearns a few days later full of anticipation . . . and a modicum of apprehension. Even though my glass is always 'half full', I still believe in the realities of 'sod's law'!

The plan was the same as it had always been. Just be myself, with no airs and graces, and try to relax while trying to sell this golf experience. After all, there was absolutely nothing to lose and everything to gain and . . . if they didn't like what I had to offer, well . . . fuck them! I'd seen and been dragged through too much shit in the great business world to be heartbroken by another enterprise knock-back!

As I passed East Kilbride, pleasantly surprised and pleased that I hadn't got lost yet, I wondered if I would meet the attached pro Alastair Forsyth—who, a bit like me, just needed a good break—to see him climb the order of merit on the pro tour. Stephen McAllister was also linked to the Mearns Academy and a past pro tour golfer.

It wasn't long before I somehow found myself approaching Newton Mearns with some time to spare. My navigational skills were either improving or I was just having a lucky day. It turned out to be a lucky day because I managed to take a wrong turn somewhere, and I ended up doing my usual sightseeing trip before, eventually, locating the golf course.

The town of Newton Mearns is generally recognised as being an affluent area of Glasgow, and some of the cars in the club car park were testament to that fact.

I parked up and began getting my gear organised when a fancy four by four drew in and parked nearby. I pulled my hickories out of the boot along with my collection of exhibit golf balls and started towards the academy to be met by a courteous 'good morning' from Alastair Forsyth himself.

Inquisitive eyes were busy sussing out the place, even though a thorough examination of the course and other facilities would be required just to see if a 'hickory' package would be practical or even feasible. It was quite plausible that on this day perhaps I would be the one to kick ass and dish out the knock-back to Mearns Academy if '*they*' didn't fit the bill.

The interior of the academy building was quite impressive—a modern building of steel construction, with a high open ceiling space giving an airy atmosphere and a large sales space below. I wandered into the dining area as I could smell a cup of tea in the vicinity. The girl behind the bar asked if she could help. 'My name's Alfie Ward, and I'm here to meet with Satty Singh, but a cuppa would be nice, please,' I said, with the customary smile.

'No problem, sir. And I'll let them know in the office that you're here,' she replied. I gave an appreciative nod and took my cuppa to a window seat.

From there I could see the driving range and an interesting putting area with the 9th green of the course behind. I already knew that the nine hole course wasn't one of the big boomer variety typical of the modern trend. The yardage was moderate and the ladies' tees were always convenient for the purposes of trimming down a few unwanted yards, which favoured my raison d'être for hickory play.

A couple of minutes elapsed before the very amiable Satty Singh and past tour professional Stephen McAllister approached me and introduced themselves. Although I had never met Stephen before, I knew him as a spectator at the various pro events Harry and I had attended in the past. We sat and talked golf and its history, with me pitching the hickory game and the possibilities of doing some business at Newton Mearns.

I explained that before any real progress could be made I would have to walk and play some golf round the course just to assess if the idea was practical for this course. Both agreed that I should do just that and then come back in to see them later. I headed off for the first tee with my pencil bag over my shoulder, hoping that I wasn't about to embarrass myself by hitting a sclaffed drive off the tee with inquisitive eyes probably watching me discreetly.

A wee quick warm-up series of practice swings with the brassie and I was as ready as I would ever be. C'mon, Freddie, nice and slow, and let's get this show on the road. The first hole was a short par 4 downhill and hardly intimidating, even for a numpty like me. Perhaps this was going to be a rare good day because the gutty ball found the centre of the clubhead and sailed off it with consummate ease and flew straight down the middle of the fairway (yes, fairway) and not a sheep or any of their shitty deposits in sight.

I picked up my tee while having a wee sly glance back towards the academy to see if anybody was watching. Bugger! A good shot and only myself to appreciate the craft of 'real' golf! Far and sure. Well, sure at least.

I'd only played one shot, but already I found myself relaxing and having fun as I chased down the fairway. Isn't this sport just fucking marvellous?! I was feeling hyper and free (just like Scotland should feel), and then a thought occurred to me as I approached my ball patiently awaiting the stroke of a mashie niblick—I wish Harry was here with me. He wasn't! So a well-executed mashie niblick found the heart of the green, where I proceeded to three putt as is the norm for me. Peter Alliss who has the car registration number '3 PUTT' would be hard pushed to be more shit at putting than me.

I continued to plot my way round the course which was proving to be satisfactory for the hickory game, except for the fact that there were several very heavy rough areas which equated to a potential loss of gutty balls by errant golfers. This could be a problem, whereas at Arbory it wasn't.

I had an agreement with the kids who played free golf at Arbory to return any of my gutties found on the course, and I would often find some myself when working on the course. Good honest customers too would often tell me when they'd found a ball and added it to their complement of five. A ball lost at Newton Mearns, or anywhere else for that matter, would be a ball lost forever!

I soldiered on to the ninth green, happy and content with what I'd seen so far. The brain was in overdrive at the sight of the practice putting green and all the driving range bays on offer. This place seemed ideal for the hickory experience I had in mind. I just had to convince the management of the practicalities and feasibility of latching on to the academy and its facilities. I headed back into the academy to meet with Satty and Stephen for the final showdown. This would be interesting.

Back inside the academy, I was ushered into the small office area where Satty was waiting for me with his two youthful marketing staff. 'Well, Alfie, how did you get on?' Satty asked.

'Aye! That was good fun, and most crucially, I don't see any problems in doing the hickory experience here,' I replied.

'That's great, Alfie. So what do you propose or suggest we can do with this?' he continued.

'Well, Satty . . .' And then I went into one. Apart from trying to explain the essence of what the experience was all about, I had to stress upon a few vital points. It appeared that I had finally managed to get my foot inside a welcoming door at the academy, and now I would have to make them an offer that they simply couldn't afford to pass up.

I put it to them, in no uncertain ways, that I was skint and couldn't invest a single penny in marketing or advertising the experience. They had the course with its fine facilities and essentially (I hoped) the customers. If they could canvass their own customers and drum up some business, then everything else would be supplied by myself—clubs and balls and historical chit-chat. I even offered a free four-to-eight ball group as a trial run just to get us going. All I had to do now was go home and wait for some bookings to roll in.

So I waited and waited and then made a couple of follow-up calls just to see if they were still on board. They said they were, so I waited and waited, till I just lost interest completely. The established businesses always appear to have . . . bigger fish to fry? Shit happens, I suppose.

The New Deal turned out to be no big deal at all. The scheme ran out, and I returned to full-time work back in my beloved building trade. Inevitably, I lost touch with Gerry, but never forgot his help and belief in a lost cause.

Throughout the world, you get the 'doers' and the 'talkers'. I like to think of us Wards as 'doers'—always have been, each and every one. Sometimes you have to wheel your own barrow, and this is just such an occasion. Take oor Tam, for example. He is probably one of the most regarded voluntary archaeologists in Scotland. A right bossy bastard like myself—he taught me a lot on our exploits for the Biggar Museum Trust.

He's made *massive* finds in local archaeology over many years now with his team of volunteers and has deservedly received recognition by way of an MBE! Then there's Grace, the solitary sister, who could 'talk the hind legs aff a dunkey'! She's the artist in the family, and a bloody good one too. She's always telling us that her artwork will only become valuable when she 'kicks the bucket'. Well, we don't want that—but alternatively we could all do with some extra cash from an art sale.

My eldest brother, John, died a few years back quite suddenly. He was a heavy plant machine driver and a real character. I only knew John, or Jock as he was called, from his visits back to Biggar to see Mum and Dad or at weddings and funerals. He was a true family man and sadly missed. And then there's Pat, the adventurer. Pat was like a father to me as I was the youngest and he was still at home. He taught me all the games you can think of during the long winter months, including chess. When he left home as a young man, he joined the parachute regiment but was forced out due to an unfortunate ankle injury. As a fill-in job, he was a painter on the Forth Railway Bridge, one end to the other—and then back again! He was a sport parachutist at Auchterarder near Perth, where he conned me into making my one and only jump. I nearly landed on the hangar roof, and that put paid to my nerves—but what a marvellous experience! Vertigo (what vertigo?)! A highly knowledgeable and a more likeable man you'll never meet.

Oh aye. New Deal? I suppose I just had to let that one go!

A Field Is a Field Is a Field Is a Field

Many years ago, Harry and I had organised a golfing trip to Eire for a group of Biggar golf club members. We called ourselves the '36' Club, and we'd already had several highly successful weekend trips under our belt. One of the courses we played in Ireland was Pat Ruddy's European course forty miles south of Dublin—a link's masterpiece which has evolved over some twenty years into a world classic course! I remember reading somewhere that Pat had scrutinised every field on the Irish landscape in search of his dream course and project and found it at Brittas Bay, County Wicklow. He was visualising golf courses in the fields all over Ireland.

The '36' Club had been very fortunate in being some of the first golfers to play The European in its original virgin state before Pat began tinkering with the course in search for perfection. But we all know, and I'm sure Pat does too, that perfection doesn't exist—right? The only problem we had that glorious summer day was when we arrived at the course. The clubhouse facilities were quite modest at that time, but greater concerns were being raised due to the fact that *there wisnae any booze* in the clubhouse! All this lot, including myself and Harry, liked a right good *responsible* gargle on our trips away, and most of us needed *a hair of the dog* that Saturday morning. A mutiny in the county was looming until our coach driver and namesake, Noel Ward, came to the rescue and set off in pursuit of a carry oot consisting of a couple of gallons of Guinness and some spirits for the 19th hole.

Neither Harry nor I ever imagined we would ever have anything in common with Pat and his golfing dream and apparent obsession with barren fields, even though *our* fields were in a different scale, type of topography, and size of enterprise compared to The European. But that's exactly how it all turned out! Nowadays, it doesn't matter whether either of us is on his travel; we're both afflicted with the *golf course syndrome* where potential hickory courses are probed from each and every landscape. Crazy—but true!

'Are ye sure this is a sensible thing to do? I'm not so sure about this,' Harry asked with obvious anxiety.

'Och aye. You'll be fine and I'm here to hold your hand,' I said jokingly. 'We need to do this and get the box ticked, Harry. I think this is what they call closure.'

We were approaching Arbory Braes together from the Wandel Bridge B Road for the first time in twelve years. The weather was pleasantly sunny on this June day in 2013. There was little doubt that both of us were deeply apprehensive about this reconciliation with an old friend regardless of any humour we tried to instil into the equation.

As we approached Coldchapel farm, about a modern drive and wedge with a *bullet* from the course, Harry drew the car to a stop. Some drivelling chatter was made related to the farm, which we had become familiar with but . . . he was actually stalling. Normally, my impatience would have told him to get a bloody move on, but on this particular occasion, the situation was different, acceptable, and mutual.

Harry was in control of both the car and our emotions, and I just let him take his own time to start up and move on towards the course. We stopped again at the north end of the course and looked out on to what once was the fifth tee (what tee?) and fairway (what fairway?) before continuing as though we were following a funeral cortège. Things were going to get tougher, and we both sat in silence for the 500-yard drive along to the hub of belated activity.

'Open the gate, Alfie. I'm going to take the car up on to the course,' he requested in a sombre tone as we arrived at the pavilion's (what pavilion?) entrance.

I dutifully obliged, closing it behind me, and walked up to the seventh green (what green?) where he had parked up. Harry got out of the car, and we stood together for only a very brief spell before we embarked on our own private surveys of the *field* under our feet. Nobody had to tell us that we needed our own space, initially, as the anticipated shock waves started stirring reminiscing emotions and venting tear ducts. I found myself wanting to scream it out as loud as I could, but soliloquised instead, 'Bastards!'

After about ten minutes, we re-engaged at the burnt-out remnants of our wee pavilion where I felt a combined choking sensation with Harry—so without hesitation I said, 'C'mon, we'll take a walk up to the top of the course and see if any ghosts appear. Maybe R. Tom Morris or Davy Syme will be playing the first?' There wasn't any point in glowering over our cremated pavilion and getting ourselves all sullen with depression. This was gettin' heavy . . . man!

We strolled over to the ninth green and the adjacent first tee. No 500 yard to half mile walks to the next tee on our wee course as is the wearisome case today. When you finished putting on any green, you only had a very short walk to the next tee! Long balls make for long walks! A short debate ensued as to where the bloody green actually was, because any distinct outline had long since vanished courtesy of old Mother Nature.

The tees, on the other hand, had all been built up using the scrapings off the greens and will remain definable for some time to come, just like the tees and greens at Leadhills and Crawford. The first tee was another story. We stood there aghast, staring at clumps of rushes that had sprung up from the ground to knee height, rendering this teeing ground useless!

I think both of us had settled down by this time and the initial shock was over, at least it was for the moment. Onwards and upwards, we started to pick our way through those boggy parts leading up to the first green, and I told Harry of the day when I had nearly killed old Davy. On reaching the high ground, we turned round and surveyed the panoramic view of the course and the surrounding hills.

It was just as it had always been. Beautiful, scenic, and wee Arbory golf course was still there, before our eyes, but only from a distance! As we searched close up for the first green, Harry noticed a solitary white peg standing all alone in defiance, which once marked the out-of-bounds area to the right of the green—one peg of around twenty or so.

I looked for the sand boxes we'd made for each tee, but there were only a few scraps of broken timber scattered about, and then I walked over to where Davy Syme's seat should have been. It was gone too with just one leg support slanting out of the ground as a final marker of its existence. The coos and the sheep had destroyed our golfing props by using them as scratching posts. The first green itself had been used by the farmhands as a good flat area in which to plant a metal feeding station for the sheep and those muckle coos! Dead fodder lay two inches deep, covering the entire green.

As we scanned the ground, *our* field was still crying out to us, '*I wanabe a wee golf course.*' Well, ye cannae be. Shut up! We tried for you, but it didn't work out—*our toils obscure, an' a' that.* The lords of the land were bereft of . . . vision and a little effort. I asked Harry what he wanted to do because we'd been there long enough. Not because this experience was still heavy, man, but because we had a rare game of golf looming at Cadrona near Peebles, and time was pressing.

'Why don't we walk along to the third green and make our way down from there?' he replied in an upbeat manner.

'Aye. Let's go. And we'll inspect your pond at the eighth,' I said. Once we got to the green, the same process was repeated.

'Where the bloody hell is it?' he asked. 'I know it was here, but there's not a trace of its outline. Ah remember you gave me a row for cutting an apron round the outside fringe. Ya big shite!'

We both laughed, and I retorted back, 'Ah well. Ye deserved it. There wisnae any fancy aprons a hundred years back, so there shouldn't have been now. Anyway, you got your way wi' the bloody ponds!'

'Aye. Ah suppose so.'

At this elevated position, we could look down upon his pond (what pond?). It had been leaking water and was almost dried up and completely overgrown with pond weed with only an eyelet peeking through the growth and showing signs of water.

'You know, Alfie, from what I've seen, it's not all that bad, is it? What would it take to get the course back again?'

'Aw, Christ! Here we go again. Are ye serious? Don't forget that this is exactly how you started the whole bloody show off all those years ago up at Roberton. Déjà vu!'

'Hmm. Maybe so. But what *would* it take?'

We began walking down the hill to the pond, and before we knew it, we were brainstorming again. 'Actually, Harry, it wouldn't take a great deal and a lot less than the first time round. That's the great thing about a nine hole course, you know.'

'What's that?'

'Well, you should learn from the first nine that you play, and if ye've got a brain in your heid, you should score better next time around. This place isn't any different. We've played the first nine. Maybe it's time we played the second round. Eh?'

Brain cells in hibernation for so long were reawakened as we walked down into the gully where a squinty sleeper bridge allowed us to cross over the trickling ditch without having to jump. Harry recalled sitting on that same sleeper bridge with Hazel Irvine after the BBC film shoot and chatting away the last of a great day.

We went up over the small incline and past the sixth green and down to the pavilion ruins once more. This wee dirty Scottish field had been virtually ours, for a short while, and we'd successfully tamed nature into a temporary corner. But those bloody moles were back, and there were casts all over the place. I wondered if Duncan still had the same old mole catcher. We went over to revisit those charred foundations, and the choking returned. It was just too many memories there for both of us to handle, and we turned back to the car thirty feet away.

Struggling to get the words out, I looked at Harry. 'Hey! We done it! And we done it right, Harry.'

'Aye. What might have been, Brother. What should have been, eh!' And we shook hands firmly. This wasn't a golfing handshake—it was a brotherly handshake! It could have been a good and appropriate time for a man hug—but I'm not the man hug type!

We made for Biggar and a much needed cuppa before heading down to Peebles for another showdown. All day thereafter, we traded thoughts and fanciful ideas of how to raise the phoenix and do it all over again.

But that old thorn was still stabbing into our sides like an unforgiving needle—it would need money that neither of us had.

Mind you, nothing is impossible. You should never discount the possibilities . . . of an impossibility. The best thing that came out of this day and its dismal exercise was that we both agreed wholeheartedly that we were glad to have got it out of the way. We had both, successfully, ticked this box.

Closure? Well, I'm not too sure about that, but we both knew that the worst of the emotional pain was now behind us and that return trips to our wee *field* that was dear old Arbory Braes would be less . . . heavy, man.

Don't Be Bitter—Be Careful

So what went all so disastrously wrong with a wee enterprising golf business in dearest Scotland? Well, let's see. The entire concept worked and possessed the feasibility required to operate as a business. It also possessed that much desired *unique selling point* to help impress upon those penny wise funding investors. I have absolutely no doubt about that. We weren't going to become millionaires from hickory golf—just earn an honest wage, entertain the people, and have some fun in doing so.

The business that Harry and I had tried so faithfully to develop wasn't one of your typical 'one hit' customer variety that has, sadly, become the acceptable norm in some tourism strategy businesses. You know the attitude that'll do them—there's plenty more where they came from, exactly like the disillusioned Smiths from England, although I have to say that our *Service, Service, Service* (in Scotland) is definitely improving.

Recent research unveils that golf generates over £1 billion to the Scottish economy every year through our vast variety of more than 600 golf courses. Absolutely bloody marvellous! Yet there was only one Arbory Braes.

Even at that early stage of a wee picture attraction with its miserly budget, people were already making those repeat visits, proving that with a bit more investment and better visitor numbers we could realise that bigger picture in the future. Mr and Mrs Hayes from Bradford had come to Arbory in 2002 on a Red Letter Days' voucher and liked it so much they came back in 2003 on my day of reckoning.

I don't think they got the best out of me that day. I knew the party was over. They would be my final customers, and Mr Hayes, a retired joiner, was the last golfer to officially play over the course on 23 May 2003. Just a few days earlier, I had taken a lovely gentleman, Mike Lister, and his daughter, Helen, from England round the course, and he sent a supportive email which concluded:

> May I wish you good fortune with your endeavours to seek the additional funding for your venture and I hope that in my retirement I will not only raise a glass to you (containing a fifteen-year-old Glenfiddich!) but once again have the pleasure of visiting your remarkable golf course.

Here's to you, Mike, and all the other believers. Slainte mhath!

A great many people got a good 'pook' out of our efforts with Arbory, Harry and myself being the only ones who didn't! Even with a shoestring budget, our set-up costs were considerable. And it didn't take long for the likes of our local rates department to get in on the act, wanting their pound of flesh, while big business got their incentive rebates. The bank too, our trusty institutions who have since had *their* wings clipped, did absolutely nothing to ease the financial pain of starting up a new business while they dished out millions in high-profile sporting sponsorships.

I suppose that's just the way it is, in business, but it was hard to accept when you looked over your shoulder at some of the other triers, all cosy in their wee fully furnished office units with the standard printer and good stock of paper, phone, and fax, etc., and all courtesy of Scottish Enterprise. And 30 per cent of them were destined to fail as well, so the statistics tell us. There could only be one conclusion for Harry and I—*we wiz robbed!*

Our timing was crap! To be hit with the controversial foot-and-mouth epidemic and the pathetic government management of the same crisis that followed was totally unforeseeable. How any government can fail to learn from a previous disaster is downright criminal! Compensation was dished out by the tens of millions to many who had suffered little or not at all. The final bill cost the country £8 billion!

And then the double whammy of the horrendous 911 atrocity! In the end, what proved critical to our success and inevitable failure was the political climate in our particular tiny niche of enterprise timing, and of course, we were pathetically underfunded!

Our great political leaders, both at local and national levels, were too busy fiddling with their own expenses and getting mired in their own brand of sleaze to be bothered with two brothers dabbling away in Scotland's under-valued tourism sector. Perhaps things will get better when Scotland becomes independent, and if the multi-national people of Scotland do say YES. Let the world know without any doubt that there is no hate or malice aimed towards any of our neighbours! That's just an ancient scam of the Unionist politicians. At least we now have an option, a say in our own future. Bring it on, Wendy Enterprise. Bring it on!

On many a day, I would walk up the first hole of our deserted course, over the ditch, and navigate my way through the boggy patch up to the green. There, up on the high ground, I would do an eyeball survey over all of what Harry and I and Ross had painstakingly restored courtesy of some blood, sweat . . . and tears. Our own little golf haven recreated for 'them and theirs', and yet there was still so much to be done! But for who?

It was a bit like viewing a crescent moon in the night sky, when you knew the whole moon was really there—sometimes you just don't get to see the whole picture.

Oh yes, there would be monuments to erect to the Morrises and others; small garden plots to create in 'out of the way' places, giving minute splashes of floral colour; more signs exalting golf's incredible history and its fantastic people; plant just a few trees here and there, a few rhododendrons for some early springtime colour; more tees would be built to give variety and relief to the existing tees; perimeter pathways would be created for non-golfers and golf buggy trips for the elderly; maybe a small practice range in the bottom fields; a big new flashy visitor centre would be required to welcome the people and cater for them properly; and more, much more—when they come.

But the actual course cannot be touched or modernised in any way; that's sacred and must remain so, in order to protect its soul! And thereafter? Well, I suppose we could then start thinking about phase two and the restoration of Roberton or Douglas or Crawford . . .

Then I would seek counsel with the Almighty, I thought as I puffed away at a fag on Davy Syme's seat. Having not an ounce of religious belief in my body, I would first ask the Big Man if Mum was OK and then enter into a 'full-on' assault of 'His' mysterious ways. He may well have created the world and all the shit within it—but 'we' had created wee Arbory and, aha, to some extent, all the shit within it too.

But there was never to be a solitary response from this great funder of the universe. Ah well, it's still good to talk, isn't it? Maybe He was just being careful.

But nobody can take it away from us—we *lived* our dream and survived every bit of crap dumped in our way and succumbed only for the want of a few thousand quid at the end of proceedings. Both Audrey and Robert have long since departed the planet, and that lottery win turned out to be a complete waste of good fortune! *Shrouds dinnae huv pockets!* The dream inevitably took its toll on family relationships, and my marriage broke up. I had hurt a few people, but that's the way it goes, isn't it? Life's too short.

However, fate is a funny character as I now happily share my life with my new partner Moira, who gives great support and encouragement. As for Harry and I, well, we eventually met up again . . . at a funeral, as you do! It turned out that he'd been virtually squeezed out of the business by . . . well, who cares now, and you can probably guess anyway! All water under the bridge. So we now share various work projects in the building game merely to see us through to retirement—but we're still here, sitting . . . waiting . . . for some bugger to come forward who isn't so fucking careful with their dosh. Then we'll show em'!

Why is it that those who have the money always necessitate the urge to be careful when making an investment or getting some long needed job done—people with (proverbially) money to burn? So many times I've heard that cliché now, and it really pisses me off! I suppose it was the same for Wallace in his day. A commoner by title, courtesy of those who had the land and the dosh, he was the true hero of Scotland, striving and struggling for what he believed in—a free and independent Scotland during bloody times. And on the sidelines sat the Bruce—watching, waiting, and being fucking careful!

I think James Dodson may have been right when he flattered me by stating that we had '*unearthed the soul of golf*'. Only those who had honoured us by coming to the course can verify such a flamboyant claim, but our vision had been realised in almost every way imaginable excepting the unaffordable luxurious add-ons of the future and, of course, the success we think we deserved.

This was golf as it was—raw and pure, what it still is in some ways, and how it should be in regard to humanity. The humanity inherent within the sport was in evidence every time someone played or just visited this course. Golfers could see the reasoning behind such an historical venture, but alas, those people of enterprise funding could not! No vision?

We had even outshone those blazers at the R&A with their pretentious remit to '*preserve and protect*' the sport of golf. They have been found wanting in this respect for decades while we had made an impression on golfers and their mindset in such a short time span . . . There are other opinions on the matter—shhhhhhh!

And what of that hickory project near St Andrews? Well a nine hole course *was* laid out at Kingarrock near Cupar, where you'll find the amiable David Anderson and his wife, Michelle, there to entertain you. It's the nearest thing you'll find to Arbory and with the same accent on having fun at a leisurely pace. The challenge awaits the adventurous golfer. Good luck to them!

Writing this book hasn't been the easiest thing I've ever done. There's been a good deal of soul-searching as I scribbled my way through the highs but most particularly . . . the lows. The context herein was meant to contain far more golf, the speciality of the sport, and its history—*a good walk spoiled* on this occasion? Luckily, I had the foresight to diarise most of our affair with golf and its history.

I had mustered literally scores of files over eight years relating to every aspect of this adventure. Each and every little snippet of information released reminiscences and emotions of our ill-fated journey. Now and again, I'll dig out the visitors' book and digest the complimentary remarks of those wonderful customers—the golfers. And as for those caustic letters sent to Scotland's *golfing* infidels—well, ha ha, methinks I doth protest too much sometimes.

So now that we've finally got this damned book chapped out—I'm thinking perhaps it's time. Yes, perhaps it *is* time now . . . to let it all go—once and for all. Maybe those business people were right when they said, 'You have to learn to let it go, Alfie.'

Then again—hell . . . maybe not!

If for nothing else, our little twenty-five acre plot of golfing history was worthwhile in creating thousands of happy memories for those who had graced the slopes of Arbory Braes in the relatively short time before her premature demise. In the words of one customer, Peter Craigon of Auchterarder golf club, who wrote in the visitor book: '*Of all the courses I have ever played—and there have been over 300 in my lifetime, I will remember this one above them all!*'

Hindsight is a marvellous thing, and we discovered far too late in the proceedings that you really had to be streetwise in so many areas of starting up a business. There were far too many things that neither Harry nor I was sharp enough to take advantage of. Funding opportunities now exist in areas where they did not, prior to the foot-and-mouth outbreak.

This time, at least, the politicians and their monkeys have learnt from such a disaster, and things will be very different when the next outbreak occurs, as indeed it will! Tourism is now appreciated not only in Scotland but also in the United Kingdom as a whole for its valuable contribution to the economy. C'est la vie!

Although we enjoyed and shared many satisfying moments during the creation of our Arbory Braes, Harry and I never really got the chance to bask in our own glory of having persevered through all the crap of making the try and having actually fulfilled the dream of completing the restoration of the course. That has to be a great pity and will remain so in my mind and heart for the entirety of my life. But I'm not bitter. Oh no, no, not at all.

Life's too short. Yer a long time deid! But no matter what our afflictions or grievances with life may be, there are always others who are much worse off than ourselves. We should never forget that. But I think most of us . . . do, don't we?

As I have a late reprieve from the keyboard again, I puff away and look up at the evening summer sky, and the stars are just beginning to shine through the dimming daylight. It will soon be the longest day in Scotland and it's 23.33 p.m. on 16 June 2013—and I'm done! The late flights to Glasgow fly overhead as they've done for years, but for the first time it's just occurred to me that, bloody hell, there will be golfers on that flight. But we'll just have to let them go! What a pity—for them.

So there you have it! A brickie and a spark and a wee golf course called Arbory Braes—joint makers of a little piece of Scottish golf history supreme. And as for all those ba . . . rascals who could have done something to keep the dream alive, but didn't—I leave Samuel Smiles, the Scottish author of *Self Help* in 1866, to have (almost) the last word:

> *Failure in any good cause is honourable . . . it is not the result that is to be regarded so much as the aim and the effort, the patience, the courage, and the endeavour with which desirable and worthy objects are pursued.*

Hell, yeah, Mr Smiles! HELL, YEAH!

The golfer's walk is the hike of a lifetime!

Alfie and Harry Ward

Timeline of Clydesdales Golf Courses

Note: (d) denotes defunct—no longer existing.

Abington: 1892-9 holes (Willie Fernie) (d)/re-opened 2000 (d)

Biggar: 1895—Langlees 9 holes (d)/1901—Heavyside 9 holes (d)/1907—Public Park 9 holes and extended to 18 holes in 1922 (present course)

Carluke: 1893—Belstane and Whitehill 9 holes (d)/1894—Langshaw 9 holes (d)/1912—Hallcraig 18 holes (present course)

Carnwath: 1907—Gallow Hill 9 holes/1922 extended to 18 holes (present course)

Carstairs: 1993—Kames 18 holes/2006 additional 9 holes (present courses)

Coalburn: 1914—Westtoun 9 holes (d)

Coalburn: 1954—Hollandbush 18 holes (present course)

Crawford: pre-1888—the Rev. C. McKune's 9 hole Glebe course/1888—extended to 18 holes by Tom Morris and Rev. C. McKune (d)/c. 1900-9 hole ladies course added (d)

Douglas: 1791–(unconfirmed) Braidley Holmes (d)/1888–Braidley Holmes 9 holes (d)/1897–Weston farm 9 holes (d)/1906–Douglas Estate Policies 6 holes (private) (d)/1921–Policies 9 holes (public) (d)

Douglas Water: 1922–Rigside 9 holes (present course)

Lanark: 1851–Lanark Moor 4 holes/pre 1898-14 holes/1898-18 holes (present course)

Leadhills (Lowthers): 1891–Broadlaw 9 holes (d)/1905–Broadlane Park 9 holes/1927–Wetbush 9 holes (d)/1935–Broadlane Park 9 holes (present course)

Lesmahagow: 1896–Muirsland 9 holes (d)

Roberton: 1892-9 holes Ladygill (Willie Fernie) (d)/1905–Meadowhead 9 holes (Willie Fernie) (d)

Symington: 1905–Angle Park 9 holes/later reduced to 6 holes (d)

Tarbrax: c. 1912–Home farm 9 holes (d)

Thankerton: 1905-9 holes (d)

Bibliography

Golf in the Making by Ian Henderson and David Stirk, Henderson and Stirk Ltd 1982 GB

Golf: History & Tradition by David Stirk, Excellent Press 1998 GB

Golf: Scotland's Game by David Hamilton, The Partick Press 1998 Scotland

The Golf Guides 1890s : *The Golf Annuals and Nisbets Golf Guide* 1907, Courtesy of Mr Archie Baird Scotland

Precious Gum by David Hamilton, The Partick Press 2004 Scotland

St Andrews & The Open Championship by David Joy, St Andrews Press 2000 Scotland

The Game of Golf by W. Park Jr Arcturus Publishing Ltd 2010 GB

Final Rounds by James Dodson, Bantam Books 1997 USA

Self Help by Samuel Smiles, St Edmundsbury Press Ltd 1997 GB

Preferred Lies by Andrew Greig, Weidenfeld & Nicolson 2006 GB

Blind Harry's Wallace by William Hamilton, Luath Press 1999 Scotland

The Future of Golf in America by Geoff Shackleford, iUniverse, Inc. 2004 USA

Harvey Penick's Little Red Book by Harvey Penick and Bud Sharke, Collins Willow 2008 GB

Poems & Songs of Robert Burns edited by James Barke, Collins London and Glasgow 1969 GB

Being a Scot by Sean Connery and Murray Grigor, Weidenfeld & Nicolson 2008 GB

Rules of the Green; Kenneth G. Chapman, Triumph Books 1997 USA

The Encyclopedia of Golf by Malcolm Campbell, Dorling Kindersley Limited 1991 GB

Golf on Gullane Hill by Archie Baird, Macdonald Lindsay Pindar plc 1985 Scotland

Biggar Golf Club: A History, 1895-1995 by Harry Ward and Alfie Ward, Wishaw Printing 1995 Scotland

World Atlas of Golf by Mark Rowlinson (updated version) Hamlyn 2003 GB

The Golfers Handbook 1967. The Golfers Handbook 1967 Scotland

I Was There. A Life in Golf by Sandy Sinclair, The Original Printing Company 2000 Glasgow

Research Sources

The Scotsman, The Glasgow Herald, Hamilton Advertiser, Biggar Museum Trust Archive, The National Library, Edinburgh, Lanark Library, The Mitchell Library, Glasgow, Hamilton Library, Lanark golf club history and minutes, Lanark Library, The Mining Museum & Library, Leadhills, Leadhills golf club minutes, Carnwath golf club minutes, Biggar golf club minutes, Lesmahagow golf club minutes.

Acknowledgements

Kelly and Ross Ward, and Dorothy: Harry, Sheila and all the Ward family: Moira: Mr Archie Baird, Aberlady: David Joy aka Tom Morris Sr, St Andrews: Dr David Hamilton, St Andrews: Neil Hunter: Graham Taylor: the Hodge family, Abington: Kevin Pilley: Chris McIntyre, USA: Sandy Jones, President of PGA: Sandy Sinclair OBE: Sir Sean Connery: Jim and Bert Reid: Davy and Anna Syme: Wayne Aaron, USA: Bill Littlejohn: Robert Leydon: John Armstrong, Solicitor: Jim Keith, Huntly: Mark Rowlinson: Ran Morrissett and Norbert Painter, www.golfclubatlas.com: Geoff Shackleford, USA: Ben Crenshaw, USA: Ronnie and Myra Aitken: Willie and Christine Paul: Ronnie (and Jane) Erskine, jiner: John Gibson: Ian and Jan Warnock, for patiently storing our sets of hickory clubs awaiting the rise of the phoenix: Red Letter Days' gift experiences and Frazer Blyth: Pro Sports Promotions Ltd: the late Bob Labbance and members of the US & British Golf Collectors Society: the BBC, STV, and the plethora of media sources who helped spread the word.

And not to forget the hundreds of people who supported Harry and I on our seminal adventure with golf history. There are simply far too many to mention in this book! Thank you all—and may all your hooks or slices be little ones.